PENGUIN  CLASSICS

FOUNDING EDITOR: T. J. B. SPENCER
GENERAL EDITOR: STANLEY WELLS
SUPERVISORY EDITORS: PAUL EDMONDSON, STANLEY WELLS

OTHELLO

T. J. B. SPENCER, sometime Director of the Shakespeare Institute of the University of Birmingham, was the founding editor of the New Penguin Shakespeare, for which he edited both *Romeo and Juliet* and *Hamlet*.

STANLEY WELLS is Honorary President of the Shakespeare Birthplace Trust, Emeritus Professor of Shakespeare Studies at the University of Birmingham, and General Editor of the Oxford Shakespeare. His many books include *Shakespeare: For All Time*, *Shakespeare & Co.*, *Shakespeare, Sex, and Love* and *Great Shakespeare Actors*.

KENNETH MUIR was King Alfred Professor of English at the University of Liverpool. He edited *Macbeth* and *King Lear* for the Arden Shakespeare and *Troilus and Cressida* for the Oxford Shakespeare, and wrote extensively on Shakespeare and other literary topics.

TOM McALINDON is Emeritus Professor of English at the University of Hull. He is the author of six books on the drama of Shakespeare and his contemporaries, including *Shakespeare's Tudor History*, *Shakespeare's Tragic Cosmos* and *English Renaissance Tragedy*.

WILLIAM SHAKESPEARE

Othello

Edited with a Commentary by
KENNETH MUIR
Introduced by
TOM MCALINDON

PENGUIN BOOKS

PENGUIN CLASSICS

UK | USA | Canada | Ireland | Australia
India | New Zealand | South Africa

Penguin Books is part of the Penguin Random House group of companies
whose addresses can be found at global.penguinrandomhouse.com.

This edition first published in Penguin Books 1968

Reissued in the Penguin Shakespeare series 2005
Reissued in Penguin Classics 2015

003

Set in PostScript Monotype Fournier
Typeset by Palimpsest Book Production Limited, Falkirk, Stirlingshire
Printed in Great Britain by Clays Ltd, St Ives plc

ISBN: 978-0-141-39651-4

www.greenpenguin.co.uk

MIX
Paper from
responsible sources
FSC® C018179

Penguin Random House is committed to a
sustainable future for our business, our readers
and our planet. This book is made from Forest
Stewardship Council® certified paper.

Contents

General Introduction

Every play by Shakespeare is unique. This is part of his greatness. A restless and indefatigable experimenter, he moved with a rare amalgamation of artistic integrity and dedicated professionalism from one kind of drama to another. Never shackled by convention, he offered his actors the alternation between serious and comic modes from play to play, and often also within the plays themselves, that the repertory system within which he worked demanded, and which provided an invaluable stimulus to his imagination. Introductions to individual works in this series attempt to define their individuality. But there are common factors that underpin Shakespeare's career.

Nothing in his heredity offers clues to the origins of his genius. His upbringing in Stratford-upon-Avon, where he was born in 1564, was unexceptional. His mother, born Mary Arden, came from a prosperous farming family. Her father chose her as his executor over her eight sisters and his four stepchildren when she was only in her late teens, which suggests that she was of more than average practical ability. Her husband John, a glover, apparently unable to write, was nevertheless a capable businessman and loyal townsfellow, who seems to have fallen on relatively hard times in later life. He would have been brought up as a Catholic, and may have retained

Catholic sympathies, but his son subscribed publicly to Anglicanism throughout his life.

The most important formative influence on Shakespeare was his school. As the son of an alderman who became bailiff (or mayor) in 1568, he had the right to attend the town's grammar school. Here he would have received an education grounded in classical rhetoric and oratory, studying authors such as Ovid, Cicero and Quintilian, and would have been required to read, speak, write and even think in Latin from his early years. This classical education permeates Shakespeare's work from the beginning to the end of his career. It is apparent in the self-conscious classicism of plays of the early 1590s such as the tragedy of *Titus Andronicus*, *The Comedy of Errors*, and the narrative poems *Venus and Adonis* (1592–3) and *The Rape of Lucrece* (1593–4), and is still evident in his latest plays, informing the dream visions of *Pericles* and *Cymbeline* and the masque in *The Tempest*, written between 1607 and 1611. It inflects his literary style throughout his career. In his earliest writings the verse, based on the ten-syllabled, five-beat iambic pentameter, is highly patterned. Rhetorical devices deriving from classical literature, such as alliteration and antithesis, extended similes and elaborate wordplay, abound. Often, as in *Love's Labour's Lost* and *A Midsummer Night's Dream*, he uses rhyming patterns associated with lyric poetry, each line self-contained in sense, the prose as well as the verse employing elaborate figures of speech. Writing at a time of linguistic ferment, Shakespeare frequently imports Latinisms into English, coining words such as abstemious, addiction, incarnadine and adjunct. He was also heavily influenced by the eloquent translations of the Bible in both the Bishops' and the Geneva versions. As his experience grows, his verse and prose become more supple, the patterning less apparent, more ready to accommodate the rhythms of ordinary speech, more colloquial in diction, as in the speeches of the Nurse in *Romeo and Juliet*, the characterful prose of Falstaff and Hamlet's soliloquies. The effect is of increasing psychological realism, reaching its greatest heights in *Hamlet*, *Othello*, *King Lear*, *Macbeth* and *Antony and Cleopatra*. Gradually he discovered ways of adapting the regular beat of the pentameter to make it an infinitely flexible instrument for matching thought with feeling. Towards the end of his career, in plays such as *The Winter's Tale*, *Cymbeline* and *The Tempest*, he adopts a more highly mannered style, in keeping with the more overtly symbolical and emblematical mode in which he is writing.

So far as we know, Shakespeare lived in Stratford till after his marriage to Anne Hathaway, eight years his senior, in 1582. They had three children: a daughter, Susanna, born in 1583 within six months of their marriage, and twins, Hamnet and Judith, born in 1585. The next seven years of Shakespeare's life are virtually a blank. Theories that he may have been, for instance, a schoolmaster, or a lawyer, or a soldier, or a sailor, lack evidence to support them. The first reference to him in print, in Robert Greene's pamphlet *Greene's Groatsworth of Wit* of 1592, parodies a line from *Henry VI, Part III*, implying that Shakespeare was already an established playwright. It seems likely that at some unknown point after the birth of his twins he joined a theatre company and gained experience as both actor and writer in the provinces and London. The London theatres closed because of plague in 1593 and 1594; and during these years, perhaps recognizing the need for an alternative career, he wrote and published the narrative poems *Venus and Adonis* and *The Rape of Lucrece*. These are the only works we can be certain that Shakespeare himself was responsible for putting into print. Each bears the author's dedication to Henry Wriothesley, Earl of Southampton (1573–1624), the second in warmer terms than the first. Southampton, younger than Shakespeare by ten years, is the only person to whom he personally dedicated works. The Earl may have been a close friend, perhaps even the beautiful and adored young man whom Shakespeare celebrates in his *Sonnets*.

The resumption of playing after the plague years saw the founding of the Lord Chamberlain's Men, a company to which Shakespeare was to belong for the rest of his career, as actor, shareholder and playwright. No other dramatist of the period had so stable a relationship with a single company. Shakespeare knew the actors for whom he was writing and the conditions in which they performed. The permanent company was made up of around twelve to fourteen players, but one actor often played more than one role in a play and additional actors were hired as needed. Led by the tragedian Richard Burbage (1568–1619) and, initially, the comic actor Will Kemp (d. 1603), they rapidly achieved a high reputation, and when King James I succeeded Queen Elizabeth I in 1603 they were renamed as the King's Men. All the women's parts were played by boys; there is no evidence that any female role was ever played by a male actor over the age of about eighteen. Shakespeare had enough confidence in his boys to write for them long and demanding roles such as Rosalind (who, like other heroines of the romantic comedies, is disguised as a boy for much of the action) in *As You Like It*, Lady Macbeth and Cleopatra. But there are far more fathers than mothers, sons than daughters, in his plays, few if any of which require more than the company's normal complement of three or four boys.

The company played primarily in London's public playhouses – there were almost none that we know of in the rest of the country – initially in the Theatre, built in Shoreditch in 1576, and from 1599 in the Globe, on Bankside. These were wooden, more or less circular structures, open to the air, with a thrust stage surmounted by a canopy and jutting into the area where spectators who paid one penny stood, and surrounded by galleries where it was possible to be seated on payment of an additional penny. Though properties such as cauldrons, stocks, artificial trees or beds could indicate locality, there was no representational scenery. Sound effects such as flourishes of trumpets, music both martial and amorous, and accompaniments to songs were provided by the company's musicians. Actors entered through doors in the back wall of the stage. Above it was a balconied area that could represent the walls of a town (as in *King John*), or a castle (as in *Richard II*), and indeed a balcony (as in *Romeo and Juliet*). In 1609 the company also acquired the use of the Blackfriars, a smaller, indoor theatre to which admission was more expensive, and which permitted the use of more spectacular stage effects such as the descent of Jupiter on an eagle in *Cymbeline* and of goddesses in *The Tempest*. And they would frequently perform before the court in royal residences and, on their regular tours into the provinces, in non-theatrical spaces such as inns, guildhalls and the great halls of country houses.

Early in his career Shakespeare may have worked in collaboration, perhaps with Thomas Nashe (1567–c. 1601) in *Henry VI, Part I* and with George Peele (1556–96) in *Titus Andronicus*. And towards the end he collaborated with George Wilkins (*fl.* 1604–8) in *Pericles*, and with his younger colleagues Thomas Middleton (1580–1627), in *Timon of Athens*, and John Fletcher (1579–1625), in *Henry*

VIII, *The Two Noble Kinsmen* and the lost play *Cardenio*. Shakespeare's output dwindled in his last years, and he died in 1616 in Stratford, where he owned a fine house, New Place, and much land. His only son had died at the age of eleven, in 1596, and his last descendant died in 1670. New Place was destroyed in the eighteenth century but the other Stratford houses associated with his life are maintained and displayed to the public by the Shakespeare Birthplace Trust.

One of the most remarkable features of Shakespeare's plays is their intellectual and emotional scope. They span a great range from the lightest of comedies, such as *The Two Gentlemen of Verona* and *The Comedy of Errors*, to the profoundest of tragedies, such as *King Lear* and *Macbeth*. He maintained an output of around two plays a year, ringing the changes between comic and serious. All his comedies have serious elements: Shylock, in *The Merchant of Venice*, almost reaches tragic dimensions, and *Measure for Measure* is profoundly serious in its examination of moral problems. Equally, none of his tragedies is without humour: Hamlet is as witty as any of his comic heroes, *Macbeth* has its Porter, and *King Lear* its Fool. His greatest comic character, Falstaff, inhabits the history plays and *Henry V* ends with a marriage, while *Henry VI, Part III*, *Richard II* and *Richard III* culminate in the tragic deaths of their protagonists.

Although in performance Shakespeare's characters can give the impression of a superabundant reality, he is not a naturalistic dramatist. None of his plays is explicitly set in his own time. The action of few of them (except for the English histories) is set even partly in England (exceptions are *The Merry Wives of Windsor* and the Induction to *The Taming of the Shrew*). Italy is his favoured location. Most of his principal story-lines derive from printed writings; but the structuring and translation of these narratives into dramatic terms is Shakespeare's own, and he invents much additional material. Most of the plays contain elements of myth and legend, and many derive from ancient or more recent history or from romantic tales of ancient times and faraway places. All reflect his reading, often in close detail. Holinshed's *Chronicles* (1577, revised 1587), a great compendium of English, Scottish and Irish history, provided material for his English history plays. The *Lives of the Noble Grecians and Romans* by the Greek writer Plutarch, finely translated into English from the French by Sir Thomas North in 1579, provided much of the narrative material, and also a mass of verbal detail, for his plays about Roman history. Some plays are closely based on shorter individual works: *As You Like It*, for instance, on the novel *Rosalynde* (1590) by his near-contemporary Thomas Lodge (1558–1625), *The Winter's Tale* on *Pandosto* (1588) by his old rival Robert Greene (1558–92) and *Othello* on a story by the Italian Giraldi Cinthio (1504–73). And the language of his plays is permeated by the Bible, the Book of Common Prayer and the proverbial sayings of his day.

Shakespeare was popular with his contemporaries, but his commitment to the theatre and to the plays in performance is demonstrated by the fact that only about half of his plays appeared in print in his lifetime, in slim paperback volumes known as quartos, so called because they were made from printers' sheets folded twice to form four leaves (eight pages). None of them shows any sign that he was involved in their publication. For him, performance was the primary means of publication. The most frequently reprinted of his works were the non-dramatic poems – the erotic *Venus and Adonis* and the more moralistic *The Rape of Lucrece*. The *Sonnets*, which appeared in 1609, under his name but possibly without his consent, were less successful, perhaps because the vogue for sonnet sequences, which peaked in the 1590s, had passed by then. They were not reprinted until 1640, and then only in garbled form along with poems by other writers. Happily, in 1623, seven years after he died, his colleagues John Heminges (1556–1630) and Henry Condell (d. 1627) published his collected plays, including eighteen that had not previously appeared in print, in the first Folio, whose name derives from the fact that the printers' sheets were folded only once to produce two leaves (four pages). Some of the quarto editions are badly printed, and the fact that some plays exist in two, or even three, early versions creates problems for editors. These are discussed in the Account of the Text in each volume of this series.

Shakespeare's plays continued in the repertoire until the Puritans closed the theatres in 1642. When performances resumed after the Restoration of the monarchy in 1660 many of the plays were not to the taste of the times, especially because their mingling of genres and failure to meet the requirements of poetic justice offended against the dictates of neoclassicism. Some, such as *The Tempest* (changed by John Dryden and William Davenant in 1667 to suit contemporary taste), *King Lear* (to which Nahum Tate gave a happy ending in 1681) and *Richard III* (heavily adapted by Colley Cibber in 1700 as a vehicle for his own talents), were extensively rewritten; others fell into neglect. Slowly they regained their place in the repertoire, and they continued to be reprinted, but it was not until the great actor David Garrick (1717–79) organized a spectacular jubilee in Stratford in 1769 that Shakespeare began to be regarded as a transcendental genius. Garrick's idolatry prefigured the enthusiasm of critics such as Samuel Taylor Coleridge (1772–1834) and William Hazlitt (1778–1830). Gradually Shakespeare's reputation spread abroad, to Germany, America, France and to other European countries.

During the nineteenth century, though the plays were generally still performed in heavily adapted or abbreviated versions, a large body of scholarship and criticism began to amass. Partly as a result of a general swing in education away from the teaching of Greek and Roman texts and towards literature written in English, Shakespeare became the object of intensive study in schools and universities. In the theatre, important turning points were the work in England of two theatre directors, William Poel (1852–1934) and his disciple Harley Granville-Barker (1877–1946), who showed that the application of knowledge, some of it newly acquired, of early staging conditions to performance of the plays could render the original texts viable in terms of the modern theatre. During the twentieth century appreciation of Shakespeare's work, encouraged by the availability of audio, film and video versions of the plays, spread around the world to such an extent that he can now be claimed as a global author.

The influence of Shakespeare's works permeates the English language. Phrases from his plays and poems – 'a tower of strength', 'green-eyed jealousy', 'a foregone conclusion' – are on the lips of people who may never have read him. They have inspired composers of songs, orchestral music and operas; painters and sculptors; poets, novelists and film-makers. Allusions to him appear in pop songs, in advertisements and in television shows. Some of his characters – Romeo and Juliet, Falstaff, Shylock and Hamlet – have acquired mythic status. He is valued

for his humanity, his psychological insight, his wit and
humour, his lyricism, his mastery of language, his ability
to excite, surprise, move and, in the widest sense of the
word, entertain audiences. He is the greatest of poets,
but he is essentially a dramatic poet. Though his plays
have much to offer to readers, they exist fully only in
performance. In these volumes we offer individual introductions, notes on language and on specific points of the
text, suggestions for further reading and information
about how each work has been edited. In addition we
include accounts of the ways in which successive generations of interpreters and audiences have responded to
challenges and rewards offered by the plays. The Penguin
Shakespeare series aspires to remove obstacles to understanding and to make pleasurable the reading of the work
of the man who has done more than most to make us
understand what it is to be human.

                                            Stanley Wells

The Chronology of Shakespeare's Works

A few of Shakespeare's writings can be fairly precisely dated. An allusion to the Earl of Essex in the chorus to Act V of *Henry V*, for instance, could only have been written in 1599. But for many of the plays we have only vague information, such as the date of publication, which may have occurred long after composition, the date of a performance, which may not have been the first, or a list in Francis Meres's book *Palladis Tamia*, published in 1598, which tells us only that the plays listed there must have been written by that year. The chronology of the early plays is particularly difficult to establish. Not everyone would agree that the first part of *Henry VI* was written after the third, for instance, or *Romeo and Juliet* before *A Midsummer Night's Dream*. The following table is based on the 'Canon and Chronology' section in *William Shakespeare: A Textual Companion*, by Stanley Wells and Gary Taylor, with John Jowett and William Montgomery (1987), where more detailed information and discussion may be found.

The Two Gentlemen of Verona	1590–91
The Taming of the Shrew	1590–91
Henry VI, Part II	1591
Henry VI, Part III	1591

Introduction

I

Othello was written sometime between *Hamlet* and *King Lear*, possibly in 1603–4. It is a tragedy of strange beauty and remarkable power. Its beauty derives from the characters of the hero and heroine, from the unique and intense nature of their love for each other, and above all, perhaps, from the sumptuous speech style which Shakespeare fashions for the 'extravagant and wheeling stranger' (I.1.137) that is Othello. The play's power derives in the first instance from its suspense, an anticipation of disaster that commences in the opening scene and develops with ever-increasing tension until we reach the terrible crime of wife murder in Act V, scene 2. More fundamentally, its power derives from the spectacle of great goodness and great happiness wantonly destroyed: a transformation in character and fortunes of appalling extremity. Such indeed is the play's power in performance that over the centuries members of the audience have been known to cry out at key moments in rage, horror and pity.

It may be useful to approach the play by way of its full title as given in the Quarto (1622) and first Folio (1623) editions: *The Tragedy of Othello, the Moor of*

Venice. In the first place, this is a tragedy and not a problem play on such issues as racial prejudice, gender relations and the pathology of violence (although it clearly involves such matters). It is also Othello's tragedy, and not that of the innocent and virtuous young wife whom he murders with grim deliberation; nor is it the enigmatic Iago's play, although he plots and dominates the action. The suffering and death of Desdemona fill us with horrified pity, and the malignancy of Iago with wonder and dread; but the fate of Othello is so conceived as to excite all these emotions, and in greater degree. For here is a noble character who is lured by a seeming friend and driven by his own fierce heart into killing the woman whom he called 'my soul's joy' (II.1.178); who kills himself in the belief that suicide will consign him justly to Hell for all eternity – that Hell whose torments he has already experienced in the imagined loss of his wife's love and in the awareness of what he has done. Significantly, too, the play has not been called *The Tragedy of Othello and Desdemona*; for the tragic focus is on the Moor, solitary alike in his magnificence, his degradation and his despair. And his colour.

Then there is his name. In Shakespeare's source, Giraldi Cinthio's *Hecatommithi* (1565), the jealous husband is simply called 'the Moor'. Shakespeare invents for him a unique, musical name that emphasizes his status as an exotic stranger and corresponds with the rich sonority of his idiosyncratic speech style. However, by calling him also 'the Moor of Venice' Shakespeare defines him as a paradox, one in whom two opposed cultures are improbably conjoined. Being a Christian and a black African, Othello is both of and not of Venice, which was the epitome of western civilization when in the sixteenth and seventeenth centuries it was subject to the depredations of the Barbary (or Moorish) pirates from Africa and of their overlords, the Turks or 'the general enemy Ottoman' (I.3.49). (Between the Turks and the Moors, and the Moors and black Africans, no clear distinction was made in western Europe at this time.) But another name which Shakespeare gives Othello is that of 'General' (first used at I.2.36). In consequence of a pattern of wordplay on the terms 'general' and 'particular' (I.3.49, 54–5) the effect of this name is to suggest that Othello, for all his strangeness, is a representative figure, and that his particular (or domestic) tragedy has general significance. The racist Iago, who reduces him for a while to the stereotypical barbarian with savage instincts, unintentionally points to a truth about human nature which is central to the play when he moralizes glibly on '*our* raging motions' and 'the blood and baseness of *our* natures' (I.3.327, 324–5; italics added), and again when he and Othello are talking of cuckolds or 'hornèd men' (to 'put horns' on a man meant to seduce his wife): 'There's many a beast then in a populous city, | And many a civil monster' (IV.1.59–64). Perpetrator of a savage deed though he is ('O blood, blood, blood!', III.3.448), the Moor of Venice is one of us beneath the skin. His double nature is ours also; we too (as the phrase went) can 'turn Turk' (II.3.164), convert to barbarism.

For a number of reasons, this play bears less resemblance to Shakespeare's other tragedies than they do to one another. But it is worth observing that when he set about turning Cinthio's sordid tale of jealousy and murder into high tragedy Shakespeare used a basic model of the tragic hero which we can trace back through Hamlet and Brutus in *Julius Caesar* to his first tragic hero, Titus Andronicus, and beyond that to the protagonist of

Thomas Kyd's enormously influential revenge play, *The Spanish Tragedy* (*c.* 1585–90). The model is that of a noble, civilized character, greatly admired by all, who in a state of extreme perturbation – in rage, delusion, madness or near madness – commits an act or acts of extreme barbarity, and in so doing becomes for a while his own antithesis. Othello's bitter remark 'That's he that was Othello: here I am' (V.2.281) is an acknowledgement of total self-betrayal that each of these characters might have made. In each of them, including the 'gentle Brutus', Shakespeare finds 'a brute part' (the pun is Hamlet's) which contrasts vividly with the unquestioned nobility of his established character; each exemplifies the notion – expressed in *The Rape of Lucrece* (ll. 1249–50), but of substantial importance for Shakespearian tragedy as whole – that 'In men, as in a rough-grown grove, remain | Cave-keeping evils that obscurely sleep'. The extremes of potentiality which Shakespeare's tragic heroes encompass, the transformation which they undergo and the terrible life-journey they experience, become in his hands a magnifying glass through which to view the instability and the contradictions of the nature we share with them, the societies we construct and the world we inhabit.

2

Before he appears in the play the Moor is the subject of intense exchanges between three Venetians who wish to identify him simply as the base Other. Not once is he referred to as 'Othello' or 'the General'. He is 'the thick-lips', a bombastic, arrogant and undiscerning commander; a 'gross' and 'lascivious Moor' who has flouted 'the sense

of all civility'; a 'Barbary horse' or an 'old black ram'
who is now 'tupping' the beautiful daughter of a distinguished Venetian nobleman (I.1.67, 12–18, 127, 132, 112,
89–90). Although their hostility to him is not primarily
racist, racist feeling is what Iago and Roderigo stir up in
Brabantio. The senator was happy to entertain the
General and listen to his tales of war and travel; he even
loved him (or so Othello believed, I.3.127). But the
thought of his daughter's sexual union with a black man,
as imaged by Iago, now horrifies him: only 'foul charms'
and 'arts inhibited' could account, he insists, for the
flight of his daughter to 'the sooty bosom | Of such a
thing' as the Moor (I.2.70–79).

The extreme and theatrically powerful contrast
between the first scene's perspective on Othello and
what we see and hear in the next two scenes begins the
unfolding of a singularly attractive and noble character,
one endowed with dignity, courage and charm. The
Moor is unmoved when Iago, now playing the solicitous
friend, urges him to flee before Brabantio and his
followers come to arrest him: 'Not I: I must be found'
(I.2.30). The furious Brabantio's show of force he calmly
undoes with a few reasonable and mildly ironical words.
He discloses to Iago the depth and quality of his love
for 'the gentle Desdemona', his appreciation of her
incomparable worth; but he believes he is a worthy
husband, reminding Iago, with an aristocratic blend of
modesty and pride, that his royal lineage and his military record will counterbalance any official complaint
that Brabantio might make about the marriage (17–28).
His magnificent speech to the senatorial Council, telling
how he won Desdemona's love (I.3.127–69), firmly
establishes what we conventionally call his 'romantic'
nature – its compellingly attractive strangeness, its rich

emotionality; at the same time, however, it marks him out as someone who fulfils the Renaissance ideal (contemporary Italy's and England's ideal) of the hero or complete man: someone valiant but eloquent, gifted with the power to disarm, move and persuade others through the witchcraft of his tongue.

It is the mark of the archetypal hero that the community depends on him; he is its protector and saviour. The unfallen Othello conforms to this requirement more conspicuously than any other Shakespearian hero. As even Iago admits, the state lacks 'Another of his fathom ... | To lead their business' (I.1.153–4); and now that the Turks are threatening to invade Cyprus, a key outpost of Christendom, he is very much the man of the moment. But the respect in which he is held is well established. It includes a special awareness of his constancy (loyalty, steadfastness, self-control), a complex virtue greatly prized in the Renaissance. Iago recalls his astonishing calmness when 'the cannon ... hath blown his ranks into the air, | And ... from his very arm | Puffed his own brother' (III.4.130–33). Towards the end Lodovico refers to him as 'the noble Moor, whom our full senate | Call all-in-all sufficient', 'the nature ... [w]hose solid virtue | The shot of accident nor dart of chance | Could neither graze nor pierce' (IV.1.266–70). Moreover, the respect he commands is enriched and strengthened by reciprocal affection. Iago hates him but admits in soliloquy that he is of 'a constant, loving, noble nature' (II.1.279–80; cf. I.3.393). When Cassio is dismissed by Othello from his office for grave misconduct, he doesn't complain that the sentence is harsh, but instead despises himself for having 'deceive[d] so good a commander' (II.3.270–71). He has 'known him long' and 'loves him' (observes Desdemona), so that his loss of

office means far less to him than alienation from his
'dear General': his one desire is that he 'may again |
Exist and be a member of his love' (III.3.10–11, V.2.296,
III.4.107–8; italics added). Montano, the governor of
Cyprus who loses this office to Othello, might have been
expected to resent him; but he has served under him
already, says he 'commands | Like a full soldier', and
welcomes him as a 'worthy governor' (II.1.35–6, 30). In
fact Othello greets all those who welcome him to Cyprus
as his 'friends', his 'old acquaintance of this isle'; and as
if to reassure Desdemona, enthusiastically tells her that
he has 'found great love amongst them'. Shakespeare is
careful to indicate at this point that Othello gives as well
as receives love: he now values the islanders' love because
it will be extended to Desdemona ('Honey, you shall be
well desired in Cyprus'); and he immediately rebukes
himself for indulging in his own happiness and forget-
ting the ship's Master, whom he asks to be fetched and
escorted to the citadel: 'he is a good one, and his worthi-
ness | Does challenge much respect' (II.1.196–205).
Here is one of those deft little signals that in Shakespeare
can say so much; it reminds us that a powerful leader
cannot win affection as well as respect unless he himself
has a generous nature.

Two words often conjoined in *Othello* are 'love and
duty'; the word 'service', too, functions as a synonym for
'duty' in this doublet, as does 'office' or 'officer' (*officium*
being the Latin for 'duty'). In common experience, love
and duty are frequently at odds, opposites, but they can
be intimately related too, for love binds and imposes obli-
gations, and duties can be fulfilled willingly, as a labour
of love. The harmonious relation between love and duty
is hinted at in this play as the binding principle in society:
as when Lieutenant Cassio with evident truth says he

'honours' his General with 'the office of my heart'
(III.4.109–10), or when the State's 'trusty and most valiant
servitor' Montano submits his 'free duty' to the Senate
(I.3.40–41). The affectionate esteem in which the General
is held implies that he himself has achieved a harmony of
duty and love. But there are concrete signs of this achieve-
ment, in his capacity both as servant and as commander.
Although just married, he responds with 'prompt alacrity'
to the Duke's instructions to proceed immediately to
Cyprus, assuring him that he will not allow love to conflict
with his 'serious and great business' as military governor
of the island (I.3.230, 258–71). The proclamation made
on his behalf on the night of his arrival at Cyprus lays
down strict time limits to the festivities celebrating his
nuptials and the Turkish fleet's reported destruction, and
it is reinforced by the orders he gives to Cassio before
retiring to bed to consummate his marriage. When later
in the night he finds Cassio at the centre of a drunken
brawl he will not allow affection for his '[g]ood Michael'
(II.3.1) to undermine discipline: 'Cassio, I love thee, | But
nevermore be officer of mine' (242–3). Next morning,
too, we first see him not as a languorous bridegroom but
as a military commander wholly engrossed in his 'duties
to the senate' – dispatching letters to Venice and prepar-
ing to inspect the island's fortifications (III.2). When
Desdemona interferes at this point with her urgent
personal suit for Cassio's reinstatement he responds firmly
but lovingly: 'Not now, sweet Desdemon; some other
time . . . I meet the captains at the citadel' (III.3.55–9).

After this, of course, Iago gets to work and everything changes. But it is important to draw together in
this way all the details that establish Shakespeare's
conception of Othello as a man of exceptional and innate
nobility; for the horror of what follows threatens

(especially perhaps with readers, for whom the play is not always a continuous and single experience) to erase the original image of a true nobility, to obscure its partial recovery and even to call its reality in doubt, as if it had been a mere mask. And that would entail missing the tragic significance of the play: that the greatness and goodness of such a man, his achievements in his profession ('office') and in his personal life, his success and his intense happiness, can be swiftly and utterly undone; that he could sink not only from bliss to despair but also from the heights of human excellence into the very baseness of our nature. Viewed realistically, the suddenness of Othello's change is incredible. But this is drama and not narrative, and theatrical time compresses and even (in this case) cunningly cheats with real time; it is also poetic drama, where all the resources of language are mobilized to give imaginative veracity to what happens, and where symbolism tends to invest the time-bound action with a timeless quality. But apart from its swiftness, the transformation of Othello's character in itself seems too extreme for probability. This idea is registered as early as Act III, scene 4 when Desdemona tells Cassio she wouldn't recognize Othello '[w]ere he in favour [appearance] as in humour altered' (121), and more forcibly by Lodovico when he says in amazement, 'this would not be believed in Venice, | Though I should swear I saw it', and asks, 'Is this the noble Moor, whom our full senate | Call all-in-all sufficient?' (IV.1.242–3, 266–7). Shakespeare seeks in these observations not only to emphasize the extent of the transformation but also to neutralize scepticism by anticipating it. And he could count on his audience accepting such a change, not least because they shared with him a world view in which the whole of nature, including humankind, is a system of interacting opposites (elements, qualities, humours), and for that very reason is unstable and subject to swift, contrarious change. As many critics have pointed out, this is a play whose technique is informed throughout by the principle of polarity: characters are strikingly contrasted, and there is a whole network of conceptual oppositions – white/black, Christian/heathen, civilized/ barbarous, fair/foul, light/dark, angel/devil. Such a technique would naturally have reminded Elizabethan audiences of their traditional conception of the natural order as an oppositional structure in which men and things can easily 'decline' to their 'confounding contraries' (*Timon of Athens*, IV.1.20).

Awareness that change and reversal are always imminent, or may already have taken place (things are not what they seem), inculcates a sense of irony; thus irony is an instrument that the dramatist uses to prepare us for tragic change. Of all Shakespeare's tragedies, *Othello* is perhaps the most ironical. From the start, the upright and steadfast hero seems to stand on shifting ground, mistaken in his sublime confidence that he can control his destiny now as he has always done. His complete ignorance of Iago's nature and true feelings for him, and of Iago's ability to bend others to his malignant will, is fearfully apparent when we see them together at the beginning of the second scene. Given Iago's determination to undo the marriage, the circumstances of Desdemona's first appearance too are unnerving. It is Iago whom Othello appoints to bring her to the Senate to help defend their marriage. Rendered visible by stage action ('*Enter Desdemona, Iago, and attendants*', I.3.169), this irony is intensified when Othello decides that he and Desdemona should travel in separate ships to Cyprus and that Iago should be her protector: 'A man he is of

honesty and trust: | To his conveyance I assign my wife'
(281–2). Shakespeare of course is hinting not only at
Othello's ignorance of potential disaster, but also at
qualities of character that would facilitate it. It is
apparent that his nobly trusting ('free and open', 393)
nature could be a grave weakness as well as a virtue.
And the self-confidence that would have made him an
inspiring and effective leader in situations of open
conflict smacks of dangerous hubris in the present
circumstances. This is especially the case when he assures
the Duke at unnecessary length that he will not allow
'light-winged toys | Of feathered Cupid' to blind his
'speculative and officed instruments', and calls down
upon his head 'all indign and base adversities' if he does
(265–70); his expansive style stretches ominously at this
point into bombast. But there is, too, a general uneasi-
ness about the nature and circumstances of the marriage
itself, however wonderful it is in many ways. It seems a
very risky affair, a daring but vulnerable union of opposites, a 'mangled matter' (171) which the Duke has no
alternative but to sanction because of the Cyprus crisis
and whose awkward aspects he seeks with evident
embarrassment to dissolve in tinny couplets:

> When remedies are past the griefs are ended
> By seeing the worst which late on hopes depended.
> To mourn a mischief that is past and gone
> Is the next way to draw new mischief on. (200–203)

One awkwardness which seldom attracts critical attention as a flaw in the marriage may be worth mentioning;
for if Shakespeare is very reticent here, giving us little
help as interpreters, he is also (in the end) curiously
provocative. Brabantio would probably have shown

Othello the door if he had asked for Desdemona's hand;
but if the General had put his golden tongue patiently
to work (before Iago offered his poisonous image of the
union), who knows what might have happened? At any
rate, Brabantio was not given the opportunity to say 'no'.
He was 'deceive[d] ... | Past thought' (I.1.166–7) by
his gentle daughter and his noble guest, and with that
bitter thought he consigns them to the future: 'Look to
her, Moor, if thou hast eyes to see. | She has deceived
her father, and may thee.' Even to an audience ignorant
of the play's outcome, Othello's grand response could
sound ominous, almost like an epitaph: 'My life upon
her faith' (I.3.289–91). Such an audience could not guess,
of course, that it would be *his* faith that would fail, nor
in what way the deception of Brabantio would prove
fatal to the lovers. Nor would it guess that their deaths
would coincide with news that the embittered old man
died of a broken heart.

The fall of Othello is accomplished in Act III, scene
3, by general consent one of the most theatrically brilliant scenes in the whole of Shakespeare. It is essentially
a temptation scene, and as such is rooted in Judaeo-
Christian myth: behind it lie the story of Adam and Eve,
and centuries of legends, sermons and treatises on the
wiles of the devil, all of which stress that he is at his
deadliest when he appears as an 'angel of light',
presenting himself as friend and counsellor and leading
his victim into sin by making evil seem good. After he
has effected the fall of Cassio, Iago identifies himself
with this great tempter: 'When devils will their blackest
sins put on, | They do suggest at first with heavenly
shows | As I do now' (II.3.341–3). And Act III, scene
3 ends with himself and Othello enacting a naturalized
version of a kindred myth, that of the Satanic or Faustian

pact, in which the deluded mortal and the demon are bound together 'for ever' (476). But although religious myth extends the imaginative horizons of the scene, there is no question but that it is characterized above all else by a superb psychological realism. The dramatist endows the tempter with much of his own acute understanding of the human mind and heart.

Crucial to the plausibility of Iago's success in Act III, scene 3, and reinforcing its wider significance, is the preceding temptation and fall of Cassio, and the temporary disgrace of Montano, former governor of the island: a practice run, as it were, for the main action, as well as a major cog in the plot. Here we see Iago's genius for identifying and exploiting his intended victim's weak point, and the effectiveness of his pretence that he is the victim's true friend. Here for the first time we see menacing signs of the passionate nature which Othello's constancy has always kept under rigid control. Here too, in Othello's angry rebuke and in Cassio's bitter self-criticism when sobered-up, are powerful expressions of the central notion of moral transformation, every man's capacity to become his own opposite: Christian to 'turn Turk', rational man to become a beast (II.3.164–6, 283–4).

In Act III, scene 3 Iago advances carefully in two stages towards the ensnaring of Othello; with seeming hesitancy, too, moving forwards and then backwards, hinting and retracting, as if deeply reluctant (out of concern for Othello) to unfold all he knows. At the start he avoids all suggestion that Desdemona is in any sense culpable; instead, he capitalizes on Cassio's recent and unexpected misconduct, suggesting that his embarrassed departure from Desdemona when Othello appeared was sneaking and 'guilty-like' (39), and that he must be in some way at fault. Not until he convinces Othello that there might be something in this suggestion does he begin his tentative approach to the subject of adultery and Desdemona's possible guilt. Accusing himself of 'uncleanly' thoughts and 'a jealousy' that shapes imaginary faults (III.3.138, 146–7), he simultaneously inspires trust and, by his cunning choice of words, encourages the 'horrible conceit' (114) of sexual misconduct to form in Othello's mind without actually specifying it himself. His answers to Othello's now urgent questioning are presented as reflecting a heartfelt concern for Desdemona's and Othello's good name, and in particular for Othello's peace of mind: he must beware of jealousy and the intolerable agonies of uncertainty it entails. Distressed by the thought of such uncertainty, Othello has now reached the point where he is willing to discuss the possibility that Desdemona is unfaithful. This possibility he rejects, and Iago airily applauds his confidence – but then shatters it with two seemingly casual observations: adultery is commonplace among Venetian wives, their only idea of morality being to conceal their pranks from their husbands; Desdemona, too, deceived her father in marrying Othello, and seemed to fear his looks when she loved them most. Wondering and pathetic, Othello's brief (whispered?) responses to these remarks – 'Dost thou say so?', 'And so she did' – register his defeat (203, 206). Venetian wives in general are guilty of adulterous deceit; Desdemona is a Venetian wife and has practised deceit; therefore Desdemona is an adulteress. Othello is trapped in Iago's false logic, and although much more is needed to secure him in that position (Desdemona's persistent pleading on Cassio's behalf, the handkerchief and her terrified lie, Cassio's alleged dream, the eavesdropping scene), this is arguably where and how his fate is sealed.

But this is not simply an intellectual triumph on Iago's part, although he benefits from the fact that he is dealing with a man not given to introspection and logical analysis. He is Othello's perverted and low-style counterpart, a brilliant orator who, like all rhetoricians, both trained and natural, knows that the way to change the mind is to mobilize feeling in the service of ideas – change, motion and emotion are synonymous. 'I do see you're moved' he observes twice (III.3.215, 222), and with barely concealed pleasure, when he senses victory.

Much, perhaps everything, depends on the feeling of insecurity which he induces in the hitherto unshakeable Othello – fear of the unknown and unseen; the sensation of being suddenly in another world for whose dangers one is not equipped. What is new to the naturally trusting Othello is the hell of the jealous man which Iago conjures up so powerfully; the notion of a society where all wives are skilled adulteresses and where kinky lust would prompt a young woman to marry a middle-aged black, only to desert him in disgust for one of her own race and age when her desire is sated (227–31); where women and men alike are 'as hot as monkeys' in bed (400). To a simple, clean-minded stranger in such a frightening world, the hand of a long-trusted friend who is not only held to be 'of exceeding honesty' but also 'knows all qualities with a learnèd spirit | Of human dealings' (255–7) is precious. Thus the other feeling which Iago exploits is friendly love, the kind of love which imposes the painful, even dangerous, duty of being 'direct and honest' (191–3, 210–11, 375–8). So the 'sacred vow' of revenge which binds Othello and Iago at the end of the scene is a parodic ritual of blood brotherhood as well as a quasi-Satanic pact; a bond which, as all bonds do, entails duties:

I greet thy love,
Not with vain thanks, but with acceptance bounteous;
And will upon the instant put thee to't.
Within these three days let me hear thee say
That Cassio's not alive. (III.3.466–70)

Such an analysis, however, gives little sense of the emotional turbulence to which Othello is subjected in this scene and which culminates in the revenge vow: he becomes, as Iago remarks with mock concern, 'eaten up with passion' (388). He begins to welcome hatred as the only way to relieve the pain of betrayal and lost love. But he is tortured too by uncertainty: 'By the world, | I think my wife be honest [chaste], and think she is not; | I think thou art just [true], and think thou art not' (380–82). His anger rises murderously against Iago when he suspects him of slander and demands 'proof' (356–60). And when Iago tells him how the sleeping Cassio tried to top him in bed, thinking he was Desdemona, and how he wiped his beard with her handkerchief, that precious token of their love, he is set on fire with rage. He sinks to bestiality in 'I'll tear her all to pieces' (428), but at the end achieves a perverted version of the old dignity and control in the deep tones and high style of the revenge vow: 'Like to the Pontic sea, | Whose icy current and compulsive course ...' (450–59). This kind of oscillation between wild rage and a semblance of majestic control continues in Act IV and into the murder scene. So too does oscillation between hatred of Desdemona and tender, resurgent love. In this way, fragments of the original Othello survive and the partial restoration of his death scene is rendered imaginatively possible.

Nevertheless, his singularly cruel treatment of Desdemona in public and in private (striking her in the presence of their guests (IV.1.240) and treating her as a
whore), and the furious rage of the killing (in Cinthio,
Shakespeare's source, it is the ensign who kills her),
would seem to suggest that Shakespeare is determined
to place him beyond all hope of forgiveness and respect.
But we are confronted in this play with tragic art of the
most audacious and complex kind. As actors, actresses
and most critics have recognized for centuries, Othello's
suffering through all of this is so intense that our horror
at what he becomes is suffused with pity; he is manifestly
a man 'on the rack' (III.3.332), tortured by the loss of
his heaven on earth. We pity him too in anticipation of
what he will endure when the truth emerges. Said Helen
Faucit (1817–98), one of the finest of stage Desdemonas:
'I felt for *him* as well as myself, and therefore I threw
into my remonstrances all the power of passionate appeal
I could command . . . I thought of all his after-suffering,
when he should come to know how he had mistaken me!'
(cited in Rosenberg, *The Masks of 'Othello'*).

Given the nature of his crime and its closeness to the
end of the tragedy, Othello's moral recovery in the last
act is necessarily less than perfect. His claim that 'naught
did I in hate' is palpably untrue, and his description of
himself (in the same sentence) as 'an honourable
murderer' can remind us only of a brutal wounded pride
(V.2.291–2). On the other hand, this half-justification
(he does call himself a murderer, not an executioner),
given in answer to Lodovico's question 'What shall be
said to thee?', is advanced with a certain ironic percipi-
ence, as if he did not expect to be believed: 'Why,
anything: | An honourable murderer, if you will'
(290–91). This troubled response, however, must not be

allowed to obscure the fact that a process of moral
recovery does take place. It begins even before the breath
has left Desdemona's body. The perverse 'duty' of
revenge and the satisfaction of his honour seemed to
impose order and meaning on the incipient chaos of
Othello's life; but as soon as he kills her he perceives
with appalling certainty that his life is stripped of all
meaning; his sense of loss and disintegration is of cosmic
proportions (V.2.98–102). Although he clings desper-
ately for a while to the belief that she was false, a part
of him clearly longs to reinstate her as a being of incomparable worth (richer than 'entire and perfect chrysolite', 144); and that part of him acknowledges that if she
were true, then damnation – 'beneath all depth in hell'
(138) – would be the only punishment commensurate
with his crime. This feeling takes complete possession
of him when Iago is unmasked. It is expressed in
language of sublime force which confirms that he is
already suffering the anguish of the damned and that his
suffering is contingent on the greatness of his heart and
the power of his moral imagination (270–79).

The way in which the entrapped Othello threatens
near the end to 'come forth' with his sword of Spain
against all impediments and stops, only to withdraw the
threat as a 'vain boast' (V.2.251–2, 262), is another step
towards moral recovery. Indeed with its subtle blend of
heroic assertion and ironic humility his behaviour here
prepares for the great valedictory speech beginning, 'Soft
you; a word or two before you go' (334–52). Justifiable
pride and necessary humility conjoin in the second
sentence of this speech: he has done the state '*some
service*', but will say no more of that, for he has to
acknowledge in himself the base Indian who threw away
a priceless pearl, and the malignant Turk who wronged

Venice and a Venetian. But then humility and pride are
reconciled, and boasting becomes an honour (I.2.20): for
a noble deed of long ago is not only recalled but re-
enacted, deed matching word as the sword – another
sword of Spain, perhaps, just such a weapon as drove
the Moors out of Europe – is turned in punishment
against himself:

> Set you down this:
> And say, besides, that in Aleppo once
> Where a malignant and a turbanèd Turk
> Beat a Venetian and traduced the state,
> I took by th'throat the circumcisèd dog
> And smote him thus.
> *He stabs himself* (V.2.347–52)

Othello's claim in this speech that he was 'not easily
jealous but, being wrought, | Perplexed in the extreme'
(341–2) has been greeted with scepticism by many; but
the claim is supported by someone well acquainted with
jealousy and suspiciousness, and unlikely to flatter
Othello in soliloquy. His nature, says Iago, is 'free and
open', he 'thinks men honest that but seem to be so', and
in consequence he 'will as tenderly be led by th'nose |
As asses are' (I.3.393–6). Emilia claims that the monster
jealousy is begot and born on itself (III.4.157–8), but in
Othello's case, says Iago, it is he (Iago) who 'bring[s]
this monstrous birth to the world's light' (I.3.398).

Othello's assertion in this, his final speech, that he
'loved not wisely, but too well' (V.2.340) has also been
greeted sceptically. But if it merits scepticism, so too
does the claim of Timon, the great philanthropist whose
boundless bounty undoes him and turns his love of his
fellow men into a raging hatred: 'Unwisely, not ignobly,

have I given' (*Timon of Athens*, II.2.179). Yet the
compassionate exclamation that Timon's change inspires
in his long-suffering steward precludes a negative
response to his claim: 'Poor honest lord, brought low by
his own heart, | Undone by goodness!' (IV.2.37–8). The
extremity of Othello's love and of Desdemona's kindness is the means by which Iago (as he himself intimates)
brings them down. Most of Shakespeare's tragic characters incline towards Apemantus' description of Timon:
'The middle of humanity thou never knewest, but the
extremity of both ends' (IV.3.302–3).

     T. S. Eliot has famously claimed, and F. R. Leavis and
many others have reaffirmed, that in his final speech
Othello is simply cheering himself up; that he is escaping
from morality by adopting an aesthetic attitude and
playing the noble hero he never really was, utterly
forgetful of Desdemona. It is possible to argue this case
with a high degree of persuasiveness. But someone who
is committing suicide and consigning himself (he
believes) to Hell is hardly cheering himself up. Moreover,
Othello is surrendering his soul to snatching fiends
(V.2.138, 273) precisely because of what he has done to
Desdemona (here imaged as the lost pearl and the
wronged Venetian). What Eliot calls 'aesthetic', moreover, is not something that Othello is turning on, acutely
self-conscious though he is here; it is the kind of poetry
in which Shakespeare from the start articulated his
conception of the noble and exotic stranger, whose original self Shakespeare wishes to recall at the end. Further-
more, to dismiss a heightened self-awareness at the
moment of death as self-deceiving egotism is historically
misguided. It disregards not only the Stoic tradition as
found in pagan literature (especially the tragedies of
Seneca) but also the Christianized Stoicism exemplified

in the political executions, martyrdoms and martyrologies
of the sixteenth century. In such contexts theatricality
signifies an admirable attempt to die as one ought, faithful
to one's values and one's highest self-conception. The
narratives of execution in John Foxe's *Book of Martyrs*
(1563), as their accompanying woodcuts in the famous
1570 edition vividly indicate, are as theatrical as anything
in Seneca or Shakespeare ('Play the man, Master Ridley,'
said one famous martyr – Bishop Latimer – to another
as they went to the stake); no less theatrical too was the
carefully studied manner in which Mary Queen of Scots
and many other persons of high rank met their end on
the scaffold in Tudor-Jacobean England. It was an age in
which Malcolm's comment on the death of the first Thane
of Cawdor carried singular resonance: 'Nothing in his
life | Became him like the leaving it' (*Macbeth*, I.4.8–9).

The negative judgement on Othello contained in the
Eliot line of criticism should be tested carefully against
the judgements passed on him in the last scene. The only
one of importance to criticize him there (apart from
himself) is Emilia. Her fearless and ferocious condem-
nation is a heart-warming revelation of love and loyalty
to Desdemona. But it occurs in the first half of this long
scene, where it is calculated to vent and dispose of our
feelings of moral outrage. Moreover, its sheer extrava-
gance ('O gull! O dolt! | As ignorant as dirt!'
(V.2.162–3)) makes the desire for categorical judgement
seem out of place. Then there is the wounded Cassio,
whose death Othello demanded and who might be
expected to say something harsh. But his only complaint
is that Othello could possibly have suspected him of
treachery: 'Dear General, I never gave you cause' (296);
and it is clear that when Othello asks his pardon it is
already given. Moreover, when Gratiano caps the suicide

speech with the obligatory conventional judgement ('All that's spoke is marred'), Cassio says immediately: 'he was great of heart' (V.2.353, 357). More significant altogether is the attitude of the grave and authoritative Lodovico, who from the moment of his arrival in Act IV has stood for Venice itself. When he enters near the end he asks in quick succession two questions that, in conjunction, define and explain the tragedy: 'Where is this rash and most unfortunate man?' and 'Where is that viper? Bring the villain forth' (280, 282). Lodovico's position is clear: Othello has been fatally rash, and is above all else a victim of Iago's poisonous villainy. Thus he rises above judgement in yet another question to achieve a truly tragic response, seeing something inexpressibly terrible and pitiful in what the Moor has done:

> O, thou Othello, that wast once so good,
> Fallen in the practice [plot] of a damnèd slave [villain],
> What shall be said to thee? (288–90)

At the end, too, Lodovico asks the 'hellish villain' to contemplate the 'tragic loading' of the bed whereon lie his wife, her mistress and the Moor, and says: 'This is thy work.' It is not unreasonable to see here Shakespeare's indication of how the play should be interpreted, and how one should respond to it.

3

The depths of degradation to which Shakespeare brings Othello are such that some of the more ignoble passages in the text have often been omitted from stage performance. Only the very best actors have encompassed convincingly the two extremes of his character. This illustrates the importance of Iago, and in a sense explains his existence. Without someone of profound malignity and preternatural cunning the task of making Othello's transformation seem credible and pitiable would be impossible. Cunning manipulators contribute to the downfall of the noble hero in most of the other tragedies, and like Iago may exhibit a clinical interest in the process of degenerative change that they are effecting:

> Well, Brutus, thou art noble; yet I see
> Thy honourable mettle may be wrought
> From that it is disposed ... (*Julius Caesar*, I.2.305–7)

But none of the other manipulators can compare with Iago, either in subtlety or wickedness, because no other tragic hero is at first (morally as well as emotionally) 'Olympus-high' and then 'as low | As hell's from heaven' (II.1.182–3).

So important is Iago that he gets almost 300 lines more than Othello and is made so extreme in his wickedness that his oblique self-comment 'Fie, there is no such man! It is impossible' (IV.2.133) reflects Shakespeare's awareness that he too might seem incredible. Until the second half of the twentieth century he commanded even more critical attention than Othello, the obvious source of puzzlement and inquiry being his motives. In conversation with Roderigo and in his soliloquies he himself is expansive on this subject, but not very helpful. He hates the Moor, and for two reasons: because Othello promoted Cassio instead of Iago to the office of lieutenant, and because Othello may have done Iago's 'office' betwixt the sheets with Emilia (I.3.380–82). Iago is happy also to incriminate Cassio because he suspects him too of having slept with Emilia (II.1.298), and because he would like to get his office. He is unconcerned too when his plotting requires the murder of Cassio, since 'he hath a daily beauty in his life' which makes Iago 'ugly'; and, in addition, the Moor might 'unfold' him to Cassio – that is, confront Cassio directly with Iago's accusations (V.1.19–21). But Iago tosses off his alleged motives in so casual and erratic a fashion that many critics have found them unconvincing. Samuel Taylor Coleridge famously contended that he is simply the embodiment of a motiveless malignity whose motive-hunting is essentially irrelevant. It has been suggested also that his descent from the Vice, the demonic villain of the late-medieval morality plays, means that he is a hybrid character, part allegorical and part naturalistic, and that resentment and jealousy are superfluous motivations for him; Shakespeare's audience would have accepted him as a character whose whole *raison d'être* was wickedness. Perhaps the most popular explanation has been one which originated with William Hazlitt and was developed by A. C. Swinburne: what drives Iago is the desire for power over others, together with an artistic instinct which enjoys the mechanics and the excitement of plotting; thus he speaks of 'sport' and declares at the height of his scheming that 'Pleasure and action make the hours seem short' (I.3.364, 380; II.3.368). These characteristics, it might be added, are aspects of his mythical ancestry, one of the most striking features of the demonic tradition being its conception of the Evil One as mocking, sportive and histrionic.

But the argument that Iago's attack on Othello and his marriage is primarily a revenge action motivated by sexual jealousy is a strong one too. This is a motive that he is much too proud to mention to Roderigo, whom he despises. He mentions it coolly and almost parentheti-

cally in his first soliloquy (at the end of Act I), but with
much more emphasis in the next scene:

> . . . partly led to diet my revenge
> For that I do suspect the lusty Moor
> Hath leaped into my seat, the thought whereof
> Doth, like a poisonous mineral, gnaw my inwards,
> And nothing can, or shall, content my soul
> Till I am evened with him, wife for wife;
> Or failing so, yet that I put the Moor
> At least into a jealousy so strong
> That judgement cannot cure. (II.1.285–93)

Although the casual nature of the first reference to jealous
suspicion might seem to suggest that it cannot be of major
importance, and although he does not mention this motive
a third time, the intensity of expression here is striking.
Moreover, this motive clearly fits with his powerful
description in the temptation scene of the miseries of the
cuckold who 'dotes' yet 'doubts' and 'suspects', with his
recognition that 'Trifles light as air | Are to the jealous
confirmations strong | As proofs of holy writ' (III.3.168;
319–21) and with the intense satisfaction he shows when
observing Othello succumb to the disease. Clearly, he is
very well acquainted with sexual jealousy. It should be
noted that he sees himself as administering to Othello
what he suspects Othello of giving him:

> The Moor already changes with my poison.
> Dangerous conceits are in their natures poisons,
> Which at the first are scarce found to distaste,
> But, with a little act upon the blood,
> Burn like the mines of sulphur. (322–6; see also
>   IV.1.44–7)

Emilia too mentions Iago's suspicions about her and Othello (and in such a way as to confirm that they are groundless, IV.2.144–6). But we should take account of the phrase '*partly* led', and not just because it comes from him. The desire to go on milking Roderigo's purse is what gets him into the plot against Othello, Cassio and Desdemona in the first place. Moreover, the plot jumps from his head spontaneously, as if a mere extension of the 'sport' he admits to having had in fooling Roderigo, and as another challenge to his ability to manage people and circumstance. The plot continues to develop in that way, and when it unexpectedly becomes homicidal, he responds to this dangerous turn with the same delight in his own improvisatory skills.

But there is another reason why classifying the play as a tragedy of jealousy is too limiting. Jealousy is central, but it opens on to large emotional and philosophical issues. In Othello himself, as is commonly the case, jealousy is clearly an emotion where love and hate contend; and Iago insists repeatedly that he hates the man he pretends to love. This is a tragedy dominated by the two great elemental emotions, so that we might do well to emphasize Iago's hatred and his problems with love (in the large social as well as the sexual sense) rather than the problematic nature of the reasons he gives for his hatred. Shakespeare no doubt observed that some individuals are pathologically incapable of bonding with others (and so of being moved by their suffering). Iago certainly seems to be one such. But he seems also to be associated by Shakespeare with a new historical type to whom social bonds allegedly meant nothing. This type is commonly identified with Niccolò Machiavelli, the Italian who shocked and fascinated Christian Europe with his grimly realistic views on human nature and the

ethics of statecraft. The Machiavellian type is impatient
with the feudal conception of society as a quasi-familial
order and a system held together by the bonds of loyalty,
truth and affection. For him, *virtù* (audacity, strength)
and individuality are everything, and moral ideas, especially the notion of fidelity, are either crutches for the
weak or self-serving (but often necessary) pretences. As
Iago explains to Roderigo, he puts on a show of 'love
and duty' but solely for his own 'peculiar end' (I.1.60,
61); and that pretence is explicit in the temptation scene,
where he claims to voice his suspicions in order to show
his 'love and duty', and declares that the order to produce
proofs is an unpleasant 'office' which he undertakes only
because of his 'honesty and love' (III.3.192, 407–9).
Those who serve their master voluntarily and with their
heart he dismisses contemptuously as obsequious fellows
whose bonds mean bondage (I.1.44–7). This attitude in
turn tells us something about his radical incapacity for
love, which entails a willing limitation of freedom in
return for something of limitless worth. Othello invokes
such an idea when he speaks of 'humble love' (III.3.455)
and above all when he tells Iago:

> But that I love the gentle Desdemona,
> I would not my unhousèd free condition
> Put into circumscription and confine
> For the seas' worth. (I.2.25–8)

Iagoism means egoism: 'And I ... And I ... not I'
(I.1.28, 33, 60); the first person singular resounds in his
talk with Roderigo. This egoism is a kind of radical
misanthropy that subsumes misogyny and reveals itself
in a perpetual tendency towards sarcasm, mockery, belittle-
ment and debasement. He dismisses love between men

and women as animalistic self-gratification (hence the fertility of his pornographic imagination). Courtesy (the 'daily beauty' of our lives) he dismisses as hypocrisy or lechery, verbal splendour as bombast. In action as in language (though in him talk and action are one) he is the apostle and agent of degenerative change, Desdemona's reputation and Othello's character being his prime targets. 'Her name that was as fresh | As Dian's visage' becomes in Othello's eyes 'begrimed and black' (III.3.383–4), his chaste wife becomes a 'whore' (IV.2.114–19). The General exchanges his humanity for a baboon, his noble stance visibly crumbles; and his eloquence collapses into spluttering incoherence while his ensign stands over him in mocking triumph: 'Work on, | My medicine, work!' (IV.1.44–5).

When Iago tells Roderigo that he 'must show out a flag and sign of love, | Which is indeed but sign' (I.1.157–8) we are ironically reminded that he is unworthy of the office of ensign, not just that of lieutenant; for as military authors explained, the duty of the ensign-bearer was to protect the honour of the ensign or flag and in so doing that of his captain and company. Although he will make a great show of concern for Othello's honour, Iago's slanderous plot is obviously the precise opposite of what his office requires. But a more important pointer in the phrase 'flag and sign' is to the fact that Iago, in furthering his attempt to change everything, robs all signs of their accepted or intended meaning. He destabilizes language itself (defined by Ben Jonson in his *Timber, or Discoveries* (1641) as 'the instrument of society'), using it to undo bonds and make chaos come again. 'It is not words that shakes me thus', says Othello (IV.1.41), just before he collapses; but it is precisely that which shakes him. By means of his lies, equivocations and insinuations, and by frustrating the proper relationship between question and answer (a process parodied by the irritating Clown (III.1.3–28 and III.4.1–22)), Iago generates ignorance, misinterpretation and confusion all about him.

Worst of all, he projects this communicational disorder into the relationship between Othello and Desdemona. When asked by her why he speaks so faintly, instead of communicating directly his fears of cuckoldry (turned into a 'hornèd man'), Othello speaks of 'a pain upon my forehead here' (III.3.281), an equivocal expression of such fears which Desdemona interprets in the obvious (innocent) sense; this misunderstanding leads to the loss of the handkerchief, that token of love whose presence in Cassio's hand, along with Cassio's other 'gestures', Othello's 'unbookish jealousy must construe ... Quite in the wrong' during Iago's carefully staged eavesdropping scene (IV.1.101–3). Tutored by Iago ('Lie ... With her, on her, what you will', 34), Othello begins to find a deadly second sense in what Desdemona says. When, for example, he overhears her explaining to Lodovico that she would like to 'atone' (231) the 'unkind breach' (224) between Othello and his lieutenant because of 'the love I bear to Cassio' (231), her words remind him of Iago's two-backed beast and unleash in public the 'Fire and brimstone' (232) of his violent nature. When she asks 'what ignorant sin have I committed?' (IV.2.69) he thinks of 'commit adultery' (no 'ignorant sin') and so is provoked to another fiery outburst that widens the breach between them:

> Committed? O, thou public commoner!
> I should make very forges of my cheeks,
> That would to cinders burn up modesty,
> Did I but speak thy deeds. What committed? (72–5)

Understanding a fury in his words, but not the words
(IV.2.31–2), Desdemona from now until the end has no
'answers . . . But what should go by water' (102–3), just
as Othello has none but what should go by fire. So the
surge of rage that he seems to need to kill her is sparked
by his misconstruing an ambiguous, tearful response to
his assertion that Cassio cannot now be questioned
because 'his mouth is stopped' (V.2.72):

DESDEMONA
  Alas, he is betrayed, and I undone.
OTHELLO
  Out, strumpet! Weep'st thou for him to my face? (77–8)

In this final divorce between question and answer and
word and sense the work of the bond-breaker is essentially complete. It remains for him only to make his exit
after stonily refusing to answer Othello's bewildered ques-
tion: 'Will you, I pray, demand that demi-devil | Why
he hath thus ensnared my soul and body?' (298–301).

4

In her own way, Desdemona exemplifies the misleading
nature of appearances and the difficulty of knowing
another person that is central to the meaning of the play.
The 'still and quiet' maiden, 'never bold', whom her
father thought he knew so well (I.3.95, 94) turns out to
be a young woman of exceptional composure who is
prepared to 'trumpet to the world' (247) her passionate
commitment to the middle-aged Moor. The candid
declaration of physical desire in her appeal to be allowed
to join him in Cyprus is as astonishing as the elopement

itself and contrasts favourably with Othello's wordily
defensive disavowal of such (a contrast in emotional
maturity which recalls Juliet and Romeo and the heroines and heroes of the comedies). But a number of
teasing suggestions hover about this most admirable
young lady. In answer to Brabantio's question as to
whom she most owes obedience in the present company,
she speaks of a duty divided in terms of past ('hitherto')
and present: to her 'noble father' she is bound and owes
respect for having given her 'life and education', he is
the 'lord of all my duty'; but just 'so much duty' as her
mother showed to him is now 'due to the Moor, my lord'
(I.3.178–87). It could be pointed out, however, that the
distraught Brabantio has asked the wrong question, just
as he lodged the wrong complaint against Othello by
accusing him of witchcraft: the question of duty was a
problem *before* Desdemona got married (when she
showed her father less respect than was his due) rather
than now. And what about love? Some actresses have
noted the forensic coolness and lack of apologetic
concern in Desdemona's reply and have tried to miti-
gate its effect by gestural means; but it is there, and it
cannot be dissociated from the announcement of a
broken-hearted father's death that intrudes so unexpectedly in the last scene.

But it would be wrong to lean heavily on this issue.
Perhaps it is best seen as one of several hairline cracks
that Shakespeare inserts from the start into a wonder-
fully romantic and courageous relationship. It initiates
the play's focus on the effects of deceit and the unstable
nature of the love–duty concordance; and it ironically
anticipates the fatally excessive nature of Desdemona's
obedience to her second lord of duty. The same ironic
anticipation is detectable in her remark 'My heart's

subdued | Even to the very quality of my lord'; this means that she is completely in love with Othello's intrinsic character (his 'honours and his valiant parts') rather than his 'visage' (I.3.247–50), but it will acquire another significance at Cyprus.

Troubling too is the extraordinary phrase 'My downright violence and storm of fortunes' (which trumpets her love to the world (246–7)). Shakespeare is here remembering the people in Cinthio's tale who blamed Desdemon's father for giving her a name of ill omen, one based on the Greek word *dusdaimon*, meaning 'ill-fated', 'unfortunate'. The idea is picked up in Cassio's remark that Othello is 'wived ... Most fortunately' (II.1.60–61), in Othello's 'my fate would have me wive' (III.4.64), in Desdemona's reference to 'my wretched fortune' (IV.2.127) and finally in Othello's description of her when dead as an 'ill-starred wench' (V.2.270). Her name seems to have inspired in Shakespeare the sense of doomed hopes, impending entrapment and uncannily bad luck which runs throughout the play and culminates in Othello's despairing 'Who can control his fate?' (V.2.263). But 'My downright violence and storm of fortunes . . .' is a syntactically ambiguous phrase which posits a nexus or an identity of character and fate (or fortune).

Like Othello, Desdemona loved not wisely but too well; for Shakespeare, great love of its very nature rejects limit ('There's beggary in the love that can be reckoned', says Antony when Cleopatra asks, 'How much?' (*Antony and Cleopatra*, I.1.14–15)), and therein lies its tragic potential. The totality of Othello's commitment to Desdemona ('His soul is so enfettered to her love', II.3.335) means that the sudden 'revelation' that he has lost her love drives him to the verge of insanity. Desdemona's tragedy is that

the compassionate element which gives her love its individual character knows no bounds. Othello fell in love
with this (and has been accused of self-love in consequence), and the infinitely perverse Iago turns it against
them both. Noting its excess with mock approval, he tells
the demoted Cassio that he must importune 'the virtuous
Desdemona' to intervene on his behalf because she 'is
of so free, so kind, so apt, so blessed a disposition, that
she holds it *a vice in her goodness* not to do more than
she is requested' (II.3.321, 310–12; italics added). One is
reminded here and in what follows of Friar Laurence's
aphorism 'Virtue itself turns vice, being misapplied'
(*Romeo and Juliet*, II.3.17), an idea fundamental to
Shakespeare's tragic thought. Desdemona speaks
'stoutly' to her husband for Cassio, and is told that it
would be politically imprudent to reinstate him immediately but that he will be brought back on 'the safest
occasion' (III.1.43, 48). Later in the day, having been
pressed once more by Cassio, she resumes her pleading.
She will not accept her lord's suggestion that the matter
should be discussed 'some other time' (III.3.55) rather
than when he is fulfilling his duties to the Senate. Indeed
she argues the case with such remarkable charm that he
surrenders completely ('let him come when he will; | I
will deny thee nothing', 75–6); and when she leaves him
he is overwhelmed with the thought of just how
absolutely he loves her: 'Perdition catch my soul | But
I do love thee! And when I love thee not, | Chaos is
come again' (90–92). But this surrender has not been
enough for Desdemona. After Iago has prepared the
ground for gross misinterpretation she returns to the
subject of Cassio's suit on two more occasions, and with
disastrous consequences. The tragedy – chaos come
again – has been written in her affectionate, confident

and happy promise (envisaging a kind of domestic comedy) that she makes to the miserable Cassio:

>   Assure thee,
> If I do vow a friendship, I'll perform it
> To the last article. My lord shall never rest.
> I'll watch him tame and talk him out of patience;
> His bed shall seem a school, his board a shrift;
> I'll intermingle everything he does
> With Cassio's suit. Therefore be merry, Cassio,
> For thy solicitor shall rather die
> Than give thy cause away. (III.3.20–28)

In the last two acts Shakespeare negotiates a difficult balance between two potentially contradictory aspects of Desdemona's character, her courage and her loving obedience to her lord. Such is her love for Othello that even when he becomes a monstrous caricature of the tyrannical patriarch, banishing her in public from his sight and commanding her to go to bed and dismiss Emilia, she responds as a model of the quiet, submissive, early modern wife: 'Truly an obedient lady', says Lodovico (IV.1.248). Emilia is suspicious of the order to dismiss her, but Desdemona says: 'It was his bidding . . . We must *not now* displease him' (IV.3.14–16; italics added). Her attitude in this, however, is not a simple expression of obedience nor of the hope that the storm will pass if she avoids resistance. It reflects an extraordinary kind of love which, she says, 'doth so approve him | That even his stubbornness, his checks, his frowns . . . have grace and favour in them' (18–20). Emilia, however, does not approve of such loving obedience: her public refusal to obey her husband's command to 'go home' and her declaration ''Tis proper I obey him, but *not now*' (V.2.195, italics added) invite us to consider it from another perspective.

The danger in Shakespeare's presentation of Desdemona as the incarnation of loving obedience is that, although it follows the logic of tragic irony, she will seem weak and passive in the face of gross injustice; and indeed that has been the impression given in some theatrical and critical interpretations of her character. But from the moment Othello strikes her in public and she says simply 'I have not deserved this' (IV.1.241) one senses a combination of strength and dignity which becomes much more apparent when she denies his accusations in Act IV, scene 2 ('By heaven you do me wrong', 80) and Act V, scene 2 ('No, by my life and soul! | Send for the man and ask him', 49–50). That she fails to stop him is not because of passivity but because of his rock-hard conviction that she is guilty and the torrent of fiery rage to which he succumbs when she seems to weep for Cassio.

If the play were so organized that the final focus of attention were on the actual killing of Desdemona and of Emilia then we might be correct in saying that its primary emphasis is on the extent to which women are the victims of male selfishness and cruelty. Emilia's acute observations on the double standards that men uphold in their marital relations, throwing restraint on their wives while they wander abroad and 'slack their duties' in the marriage bed (IV.3.85–102), would certainly reinforce such an impression. On the other hand, Emilia remarks in the same speech that women have the same frailty as men. One of the most subtle aspects in the design of the play is the manner in which its varied and vividly contrasted characters, both male and female, evince a network of similarities that serves to emphasize the collective nature of the tragedy. The conspicuous analogy between Cassio and Othello, and the contribution of Cassio's failings to Iago's plot, have already been emphasized. But Emilia's character, too, is integral to the tragedy insofar as it is a tragedy that turns on deceit. Her love for her mistress is such that she feels 'bound to speak' (V.2.183) the truth in defiance of Iago; but it was not always thus with her love and duty. Without her very deliberate lie to Desdemona about the lost handkerchief, and her more reprehensible silence on a subsequent occasion (in both of which actions we might detect a sense of divided duty), the tragedy might never have happened. Then there is Bianca's impatient pestering of Cassio and her jealous outbursts (III.4.165–96, IV.1.148–55), which fall perfectly into Iago's plot. Brabantio, too, is a strange version of Othello. His 'particular grief | Is of so flood-gate and o'erbearing nature | That it engluts and swallows other sorrows', including 'the general care' of the state; and it is in some degree responsible for Desdemona's fatal determination to go to Cyprus rather than wait at home for Othello's return (I.3.55–7, 54, 239–41). He dies of 'pure grief' at losing her, but if he had lived to hear what happened to her (says Brabantio's brother Gratiano), it would have 'ma[d]e him do a desperate turn, | Yea, curse his better angel from his side, | And fall to reprobance' – that is, commit suicide and risk damnation (V.2.204, 206–8). Othello is assuredly more at fault than anyone except Iago, but no one is faultless in relation to the tragic sequence of events. And such are the heights from which Othello falls that his fate is more fearful than any one else's; his suffering, too, his 'pure grief', tops extremity.

5

It is commonly said that *Othello* is uniquely intense but lacks magnitude and scope, being (after Act I) a claustrophobic personal tragedy divorced from the political and cosmological contexts that lend grandeur of implication to the other tragedies. There is considerable truth in this view, but it has been overstated. The play has links with early modern politics and pre-modern natural philosophy that, being unemphatically invoked, have gone largely unnoticed, even in historically oriented criticism.

In Cinthio's novella, published in 1565, the setting is contemporary and there is no mention of war or of any immediate threat to Cyprus, nor is there a single reference to 'the Turk'. Shakespeare adds the Turkish threat and in so doing brings the action forward to what seems like a precise historical moment, that is to 1570, when the Turks sailed from Constantinople by way of Rhodes with 'a most mighty preparation' of galleys in their first and only attempt to seize Cyprus (I.3.34, 219). It has been said that the sole purpose of this political context is to establish at the outset the superior worth of the Moor and the depth of Desdemona's love (prepared as she is to follow him to war). After Act II, scene 1, when the action spirals inward from 'state affairs' to 'house affairs' and what men 'privately determine' (I.3.188, 146, 272), it seems to exist no longer.

However, this limitation on the imaginative effect of the political frame presupposes too much suspension of historical consciousness on the part of Shakespeare and his audience. Rather, it can be argued that the Turco-Christian conflict is exploited (in keeping with the prevailingly ironic and ominous mood of the tragedy) as a largely silent but eloquent presence throughout, a pointer to what '[s]ucceeds in unknown fate' (II.1.187). It is reported in Act II, scene 1 that the Turkish fleet perished in the storm, and the jubilant cry goes up twice, 'Our wars are done' (20, 196). But 'these beneficial news' (II.2.6) are not reported by an eyewitness; Montano's question 'Is this true?' (II.1.25) hangs in the air, and anyone in the audience with a moderately sensitive ear would recall the first lines of the previous scene when reports about the shifty movements of the Turks were about to be scrutinized with great care: 'There is no composition in these news | That gives them credit' (I.3.1–2). Could it be that most of the Turkish fleet is (in Montano's words) 'ensheltered and embayed' out of the storm (II.1.18) and that Othello's joyous declaration 'News, friends, our wars are done; the Turks are drowned' (196) is disqualified by what he says four lines later (apropos his forgetting to send for the ship's master): 'I prattle out of fashion and I dote | In mine own comforts' (200–201)?

Shakespeare and his contemporary audience would surely have known that the Cyprus wars were not 'done' in the play's time-world, that the Turks seized the island with characteristic ferocity at their one and only attempt (in 1570) and were still very much in possession of it. If a reminder of that fact was necessary, there was Ralph Carr's *The Mahumetane or Turkish Historie* (1600), which, as the title page promises, appends a separate 'discourse of the wars of Cyprus, at what time Selimus took from the Venetians the possession of it'. Moreover, Carr's book, like Richard Knolles' monumental *Historie of the Turkes* (1604), reflected current fears about the seemingly unstoppable seizure of Christian territories by the Turks in western Europe and elsewhere: as the anonymous author of *The Policy of the Turkish Empire* (1597) put it, 'The terror of their name doth even now make the kings and princes of the West ... to tremble and quake through fear of their victorious forces'. On the other hand, Knolles warned that while this 'barbarous nation ... now triumpheth over the best part of the world', many Christians seem lost 'in the dead sleep of careless negligence and security' (doting in their own comforts, like the General and his Cypriot friends?). Knolles and other historians and moralists, however, were agreed that the success of the Turks was not due mainly to their military might but rather to the mutual envies and treacheries of the Christians.

It would have been impossible for such knowledge and such fear not to have affected an audience's response to *Othello* at the beginning of the seventeenth century, and it seems very likely that Shakespeare intended it should. Once entertained, it compounds the sense of doom and entrapment present in Act I, scene 3, when Desdemona insists on going to Cyprus, and above all in Act II, scene 1, when Iago watches the Governor and his wife with malign intent and plots an action that '[w]ill shake this island' (II.3.123); but it emphasizes too the notion of the enemy within, the fact that not all Turks are turbaned. A '[m]ost heathenish' Christian (V.2.309), envious, treacherous Iago is the spiritual ally of intending invaders: 'Nay, it is true, or else I am a Turk' (II.1.113).

For modern audiences and readers the crucial fact about the condition of Cyprus at the end of the play is that order has been restored and Cassio installed as Othello's successor: now at least 'Heaven [will] bless the isle of Cyprus' (II.2.10–11) in answer to the Herald's prayer. However, Othello has been presented as the only man capable of holding the island against the Turks, whereas his gentlemanly lieutenant is manifestly a lightweight character. It seems probable then that the play was intended to leave its first audiences with the thought that what Iago, Roderigo and Othello 'privately determine' in their envies and jealousies, *or something very like it*, was responsible for the calamity that awaited Cyprus 'in unknown fate', fulfilling Brabantio's prediction: 'For if such actions may have passage free | Bondslaves and pagans shall our statesmen be' (I.2.98–9). If that is so, then the fictive history of Othello has been located within the tragic history of early modern Christendom – as read by contemporary observers – in such a way that it functions as a microcosm of that ongoing catastrophe, and even (by a kind of imaginative sleight of hand, which confuses fiction and history) as an important turning point in its development. In its relation to history *Othello* must have seemed a hauntingly reverberant tragedy.

6

For Shakespeare's contemporaries, Cyprus was not only a place of considerable historical and political significance; it had mythic and symbolic associations by means of which Shakespeare implicitly locates the tragedy in the natural order and hints at a matrix for all the play's polarities. When Brabantio expostulates against Iago's farmyard obscenities and declares 'This is Venice: My house is not a grange' (I.1.106–7) he introduces the antithesis of civility and barbarism that pervades the tragedy and is played out in the character of 'the Moor of Venice'. Cyprus, however, does not represent the second element in the antithesis. That symbolic role belongs to the Turk. Cyprus is located at the vulnerable edge of civilization, and as such is a place where civility, love and peace maintain a fragile hold over the forces which oppose them; it represents the underlying reality of Venice and of all cities and institutions, Christian and otherwise, where what prevails is at best a kind of *discordia concors*. Meaning 'concordant discord' or (to quote Pierre de la Primaudaye's popular sixteenth-century ency-clopaedia, *The French Academy*) 'harmonious contrariety', the phrase was a pre-modern commonplace. It was used to define the whole system of nature, the elemental order governed by sympathetic and antipathetic forces (as objectively real as electricity and magnetism are to us). These forces were identified as Love (Friendship) and Strife (War, Hatred), and their relationship was tradi-tionally figured in the myth of Mars (god of war) and Venus (goddess of love and peace): the deities from whose union was born the goddess Harmony, and whose beneficent but temporary conjunction was as familiar in astrology as in mythology. There were, however, two well-known interpretations of the Mars–Venus myth. In the first the goddess Harmony is ignored and the story is interpreted as a warning to the warrior (and every nobleman was by profession a warrior) against the shameful, self-destructive consequences of surrendering to amorous sensuality. This interpretation is invoked when Othello assures the Senate that he will not allow 'light-winged toys | Of feathered Cupid' (Venus' son) to interfere with his military duties on Cyprus (I.3.265–71). In the other interpretation, often used in aristocratic marriage masques, the goddess Harmony is all-important and the myth is treated as an allegory of the fruitful bonding of opposites in nature's *discordia concors*.

As every Renaissance poet and painter knew, Venus (or Aphrodite) was 'foam-born' and rose from the sea off Cyprus, where her cult flourished for centuries (she was often referred to in poetry as 'the Cyprian' or 'the Cyprian queen'). Thus it might seem a curious oversight on Shakespeare's part that there is no explicit reference to her in *Othello*; but in dealing with so familiar a myth Shakespeare's touch is understandably lighter than that, and his organization of the action, his metaphors and his diction make it quite clear that the birth of Venus and her short-lived union with Mars symbolically shadows the love tragedy of Othello and Desdemona. The scene of the lovers' arrival and meeting at Cyprus is carefully designed as the high point of their relationship and as the moment when their individual greatness is most fully affirmed. It seems as if all the citizens of Cyprus are assembled to greet them; but it is significant that the lovers arrive separately. 'The *divine* Desdemona' (II.1.73) is the first to step ashore, and she is greeted by Cassio with almost as much reverence as was accorded the deity herself in Cyprus of old. After an anxious delay comes 'the warlike Moor', the 'full soldier' whom 'the valiant of this warlike isle ... so approve' (27, 36, 43–4); and it is not far-fetched to suggest that 'Moor' and 'Mars' are silently equated here, for in Shakespeare (as in other poets), 'warlike' is synonymous with 'Mars' and 'martial' ('warlike and martial Talbot' (*Henry VI, Part I*, III.2.118), 'Then should the warlike Harry, like himself, | Assume the port of Mars' (*Henry V*, Prologue, 5–6)). When the pair meet and embrace they achieve a transcendent harmony in which Desdemona is associated with *Venus armata*, armed Venus, signifying in iconographic tradition the triumph of love: 'O, my fair warrior!', exclaims Othello (II.1.176). Their loving exchange too is crowned with the Moor's proclamation of friendship and peace for the whole island: 'News, friends, our wars are done' (196). It would seem that 'this warlike isle' will once more become 'this fair island' (II.3.137).

What is particularly impressive in Shakespeare's use of the Mars–Venus myth here is the ease with which he embeds it in the elemental order of nature and stresses that order's twin potential. When Desdemona is on the point of stepping ashore Cassio utters a prayer for Othello's safe arrival in which he defines the anticipated reunion of the lovers and consequent reanimation of the island in terms of the harmony of the elements (II.1.76–82). But he has already prayed that 'the heavens | Give [Othello] defence against the elements', and he will soon be telling Desdemona that '[t]he great contention of the sea and skies | Parted our fellowship' (44–5, 92–3); his phrasing echoes thus the powerful descriptions of the storm at the start of the scene as a fierce battle between wind, lightning, sea and land (1–17). Adroitly, too, the elemental ferocity of nature in these passages is linked to Iago, for 'the foul and violent tempest' (34) which separated Othello and Cassio at sea, the wind which 'speaks aloud at land' and 'hath ruffianed so upon the sea' (5–7), recalls the foul-speaking 'ruffians' who in the opening scene 'call[ed] aloud' with 'dire yell' to the sleeping Brabantio with the intention of poisoning the Moor's delight (I.1.111, 75–6, 69). Watching the lovers embrace here, and filled with hatred and envy, Iago the bond-breaker is a quiet embodiment of the destructive force in nature's and human nature's unstable order: as soon as he hears the delighted Othello pray that the kisses he exchanges with Desdemona will be 'the greatest discords ... | That e'er our hearts shall make' he mutters: 'O, you are well tuned now! | But I'll set down the pegs that make this music' (II.1.192–5). Thus Cassio will be parted once more from Othello, Desdemona will overstep the mark as 'our great Captain's Captain' (74), and Othello will endure all the 'indign and base adversities' (I.3.270) that he invoked in the Senate if he should ever allow Desdemona to interfere with his great business to the State. In short, the other version of the myth will be enacted with unprecedented grimness in an action that carries suggestions of primal chaos.

Rage and pity, fire and tears, do battle for Othello's soul and Desdemona's life. His jealousy-and-hate is the explosion of an elemental force seeking to overwhelm the force that contains it. To Emilia he says 'She was false as water', and she retorts, 'Thou art rash as fire to say | That she was false' (V.2.135–6). Indeed for him the elemental strife and confusion that his tragedy epitomizes stretches out into eternity itself, for the Hell he imagines is a formless vast where the soul is blown about in winds, roasted in sulphur and washed in 'steep-down gulfs of liquid fire' (277–8).

Thus if we attend to Shakespeare's poetry and stagecraft we can see much more than a 'private and domestic quarrel' (II.3.209) on a small island, more even than the Islamic-Christian conflicts of early modern and contemporary history. The tragedy speaks to the educated imagination about the history of humankind, about the never-ending uncertainty in the relationship between the 'fair' and the 'warlike' in all that we do and are.

Tom McAlindon

The Play in Performance

Within the limits that define its uniqueness, *Othello* has yielded in performance a great variety of effects and emphases. This variety is determined by the way in which the constituent elements of the dramatic art, both auditory and visual, have been used to give life to the words of the play-text. But, like most Shakespearian tragedies, it is seldom produced in its entirety, so cuts in the text have also been a differentiating factor.

There are, however, a number of constants in performance history, challenges which have engaged the inventiveness of succeeding generations of actors and producers. The nobility of the hero seems to have been the guiding assumption in the most successful performances, from Thomas Betterton in the late seventeenth century to the twentieth-century black actors Paul Robeson (1930, 1943), Willard White (1989), Laurence Fishburne (in Oliver Parker's 1995 film adaptation) and Ray Fearon (1999); one notable exception has been that of Laurence Olivier in a 1964 production whose programme notes signalled its indebtedness to F. R. Leavis's powerfully anti-Othello essay. This virtual unanimity on the intrinsic nobility of the hero can probably be extended to include the greatest actor of Shakespeare's age, Richard Burbage, who according to a contemporary found his 'chiefest part', that which 'moved the heart ... beyond the rest' in the character of 'the grieved Moor, made jealous by a slave'. It seems unlikely that such consensus has been due to the reluctance of famous and powerful white actors to play the part of a hero whose essential nobility was in question, or of Afro-American actors to cast a slur on their race. The more obvious reason is that they have all felt required by the text to accept the envious Iago's admission that the Moor was of a free, open and noble nature.

The first challenge to the actor playing Othello is that of reconciling the impression of a genuine nobility with the degrading passions and the brutal murder to which he descends; and most of the great actors, including Burbage, clearly deduced from the text that the solution to the problem lies in the intensity of the hero's suffering and his capacity to excite a rare degree of pity in an audience. Necessary here is an ability to master tone and gesture so as to convey rapidly fluctuating emotions, where suspicion and anger are in agonized interplay with tenderness and grief. Writing in his journal *The Tatler* (1709–11), the essayist Richard Steele indicated that Betterton captured this interplay to perfection: 'The wonderful agony [when he questions Desdemona about the handkerchief] ... the mixture of love that intruded upon his mind upon the innocent answers Desdemona makes, betrayed in his gestures such a variety and vicissitude of passion as would admonish a man to be afraid of his own heart.' The success of Spranger Barry (1719–77) and of Edmund Kean (1787–1833) in meeting this requirement was outstanding and well documented by contemporaries. In the 'brothel scene' of IV.2.1–93 (where Othello mockingly treats Desdemona as prostitute and Emila as bawd) 'the very antithesis' of Barry's rage, wrote John Bernard in *The Theatrical Review* (1772), was the manner in which (in the same scene) 'he gave the words, "O, Desdemona – away – away – away!" ... he looked a few seconds in Desdemona's face, as if to read her feelings and disprove his suspicions; then, turning away, as the adverse conviction gathered in his heart, he spoke falteringly, and gushed into tears'. Kean was admired by G. H. Lewes (1817–78) for 'the deep and haggard pathos, the forlorn sense of desolation' that alternated with his 'stormy cries for vengeance' (*On Actors and the Art of Acting* (1875)). This tradition was maintained in the Victorian period by Tommaso Salvini (1829–1915), whose Othello (wrote Emma Lazarus in *Century Magazine* 23 (1881)) 'compels our love, our admiration, our pity, our horror, and in the end our aching sympathy'; and it has been apparent in the twentieth century in (most notably) the Othellos of Paul Robeson, Anthony Quayle (1954) and Willard White. In Trevor Nunn's impressive RSC production at the Other Place in 1989 White achieved a wonderful intensity of contrary emotions in Act IV, scene 1 ('Nay, that's certain – but yet the pity of it, Iago ...' (194)) and in the brothel scene, where he wept as his terrible rage gave way to the misery of lost love, first in 'Ah, Desdemon! Away, away, away!' (IV.2.40) and then in 'But there where I have garnered up my heart ...' (56). In both scenes his rage, although terrible, was scarcely distinguishable from embittered love.

A concomitant challenge to the actor is to project the emotional extremes of Othello's character with equal force. A number of distinguished performers (including Robeson) have been either unable or unwilling to act out the full savagery of his rage. But even in the eighteenth century, when notions of decorum cut the text extensively, including those points where Othello is at his most brutal, the best actors met this challenge impressively. In Spranger Barry the audience could see 'the muscles stiffening, and the veins distending' to match the bloody passion which shakes his very frame, 'a mighty flood of passion accumulating for several minutes and sweeping . . . love, reason, mercy all before it', so that female spectators 'used invariably to shriek' (William Hazlitt, *Complete Works*, ed. P. D. Home, vol. 18 (1933)). In the Romantic period Byron and others wept at Kean's grief, but his fury left indelible memories: 'I was frightened,' wrote Lord Gower to a friend, 'alarmed . . . I wished to be away, and saw those *eyes* all night, and *hear*, "D—n her! D—n her!" still – it was too horrible' (*Private Correspondence 1781 to 1821*, ed. Castalia Countess Granville (1916); quoted in A.C. Sprague, *Shakespearian Players and Performances* (1953)). Victorian gentility constrained leading actors such as W. C. Macready and Henry Irving, but Salvini showed that rage stretching to a wild physical violence could be convincingly combined with the most affecting manifestations of love and gentleness. Few actors have communicated more powerfully Othello's love for Desdemona than Ray Fearon in our own time (RSC, 1999), yet the savagery in his treatment of her was extreme; the famous blow to her face (IV.1.240), which many before him either dropped or delivered as a tap with rolled-up paper, was given with shocking force.

Othello's collapse into jealousy in one (albeit long) scene constitutes an obvious threat to the impression of nobility as well as to plausibility, so the best actors have won praise for the slowness with which they react to Iago's hints in Act III, scene 3. Edwin Booth (1833–93), Salvini, Olivier and White all uttered 'O, misery!'

(III.3.169) not subjectively but in sympathy for the victim of jealousy described by Iago; until 'Dost thou say so?' or 'And so she did' (203, 206) Iago is usually having some difficulty in distracting Othello from his papers or maps.

Being both jocular and malevolent, the character of Iago, like that of Othello, calls for a difficult balance in the actor. Kean played this part as well as Othello and was guilty of starting a fashion for the 'gay and careless villain' (Hazlitt's phrase) devoid of the profound hatred without which his cruelty seems incomprehensible. In Tyrone Guthrie's 1938 production Olivier's homosexual Iago (allegedly rationalizing his unconscious love for the Moor as hatred) was essentially of this cast: 'a roguish skylarker', wrote Alan Dent (Rosenberg, *The Masks of 'Othello'*). In Oliver Parker's memorable film Kenneth Branagh's Iago was rather similar, a winking mischief-maker. On the other hand, Iago's malevolence must never be apparent to anyone but the audience, or Othello's ensnarement will seem improbable. Reacting against a line of scowling Iagos, Edwin Booth (one of the greatest Iagos ever) said that '[t]o portray Iago properly you must seem to be what all the characters think and say you are, not what the spectators know you to be; try to win even *them* by your sincerity. Don't *act* the villain' (Rosenberg). In the Trevor Nunn RSC production (filmed for television and video in 1990) Ian McKellen's Iago met this requirement superbly. Outside the soliloquies only his watchful silences and restless manual fidgeting with various props hinted at the destructive energies seething below the surface of rough kindliness and sportive bonhomie. There is, however, a different imbalance potential in productions with a really great Iago: the temptation is to make it seem like *his* play. In the Nunn production Lodovico's concluding promise that he 'will ... to the state | This heavy act with heavy heart relate' (V.2.366–7) was cut and instead the audience's attention was focused at the end on McKellen's prolonged, expressionless gaze as he stood tall, looking *down* on the bed and his victims (an echo of the spectacular opening shot in Orson Welles's film version (1978), where Iago looks down from his hoisted cage at the funeral procession, his eyes fixed on the dead Moor). One forgot in Nunn's ending the fact that Iago had been shocked, diminished and defeated by the power of true love. And one missed the Lodovico cadence, the residual tone of the tragedy: neither censorious nor angry, but grave and sad.

Eighteenth- and nineteenth-century standards of propriety demanded thoroughgoing excision of the sexually coarse element in Iago's language, and in that of the transformed Othello. One effect of this was to blunt the contrast in the play between two conceptions of love, another was to obscure the diseased and corrupting nature of Iago's mind as well as the unsatisfactory nature of his relationship with Emilia, both of which are strikingly obvious in contemporary productions. And although removing 'indelicacies' from Othello's speech had the secondary effect of diminishing his ignobility (or protecting his nobility), in one important instance the effect was the reverse. The removal of the 'brothel' scene, as the Victorian critic William Lloyd complained, made the bedchamber scene appear with 'all the shockingness of a contrived, cold-blooded murder' (cited in the Variorum *Othello*, ed. H. H. Furness).

Imbalances in the portrayal of Desdemona have also been a feature of performance history, though less noticeably of late. Hers is a character of delicate complexity, difficult to realize on stage and often accused of inconsistency (but see Introduction, pp. li–lii). We do

not know whether any stage business was supplied on
Shakespeare's stage to soften the effect of her speech on
a divided duty (I.3.178–87), but stage tradition since the
early nineteenth century has provided a good deal of it,
though without justifying textual pointers: she might
look apologetically to her father when she enters, attempt
unsuccessfully to embrace him, or kneel for his blessing
and be distraught by his rebuff. But such business
arguably diminishes her stature as a tragic heroine courageous and determined to excess in her dedication to the
man she loves. (It diminishes too her father's tragic
quality, so movingly elicited by Alexander Knox in the
1938 Tyrone Guthrie production: there, the old man's
heart visibly cracked, so that the news of his death delivered in the last scene was unsurprising.)

Tenderness has always been the essence of her character when well performed on stage, but she should seem
neither angelic nor excessively sweet. And as Ellen Terry
contended, she should be played by an actress of stature
and not by a relatively untalented lightweight, as has
often been the case (*Four Lectures on Shakespeare* (1932)).
She seems to submit to her 'wretched fortune' in Act IV,
but in the final impression she is not passive. Susannah
Cibber (1703–58) was the first of many Desdemonas
who protested their innocence 'with uncommon energy'.
The best Desdemonas of the nineteenth century criti-
cized those who (in Fanny Kemble's phrase) 'acquiesced
with wonderful equanimity in their assassination'; like
Helen Faucit, Kemble 'made a desperate fight for it'
(Frances Kemble, *Records of Later Life* (1882); quoted
in Rosenberg). Emphasizing the strength behind the
tenderness and charm, these actresses saw a connection
between her defiance of her father, her resolute pursuit
of Cassio's case, her physical resistance ('Nay, if you

strive', V.2.82) and her heroic-pathetic attempt to save
Othello from incrimination.

For reasons of economy and decorum, Act IV, scene
3, which includes Desdemona's willow song, Emilia's
defence of adultery at the right price and her attack on
the double standard in marital relations, was cut
throughout most of the eighteenth and nineteenth
centuries; and so in consequence was Emilia's dying 'in
music' (V.2.246). Actresses rightly lamented these exci-
sions. Performed in its entirety as it normally is today,
Act IV, scene 3 intensifies the singular pathos that
surrounds Desdemona's character. It strengthens the
theatrically compelling and obviously significant contrast between the two women, provides (in the willow
song) a deeply moving point of repose before the tragic
climax, and draws attention to what G. B. Shaw (with
reference to Emilia) called 'Shakespeare's curious anticipation of modern ideas', i.e. his feminism (*Dramatic
Opinions and Essays* (1906)). With the restoration of Act
IV, scene 3, full justice could now be done to the character of Emilia, a minor but rewarding role which many
actresses would prefer to that of Desdemona. Recent
productions, especially that of Trevor Nunn, have
emphasized her love of Iago, his contemptuous treatment of her and the pain and disillusion which lie behind
her cynical comments on men and marriage.

Paul Robeson said that Othello's colour is essentially
secondary, a means for emphasizing his cultural difference and consequent vulnerability in a society he does
not fully understand. In Robeson's performance of the
part, however, the colour difference seemed more important than that: to many observers, he appeared to carry
the historic burden of slavery and oppression from the
start, becoming himself an object of pity alone and not

of awe. Janet Suzman's passionately politicized version
of the play, performed with great courage and point in
racist South Africa in 1988, carried this tendency as far
as it might go; the racist feelings expressed by Iago,
Brabantio and Emilia become the key to the entire play.
Othello is no majestic figure, but frail and rather sad;
Iago is a towering bully modelled on Eugene Terre-
blanche, a notoriously racist Afrikaner of the time; and
even the amiable First Senator is turned into a stereo-
typed racist: his 'Here comes Brabantio and the valiant
Moor' (I.3.47) becomes a contemptuous 'Here comes the
Moor'. Available on video, this reductive but powerful
and moving production raises important questions about
legitimacy of interpretation and the constraints of the
text. It invites us to consider at what point a fresh and
inventive performance of a Shakespeare play trans-
gresses the limits that define its uniqueness and becomes
instead an adaptation.

A notable feature of the 2004 RSC production at the Swan
Theatre in Stratford-upon-Avon, directed by Gregory
Doran, was the performance of the South African actor
Sello Maakeka Ncube in the title role, arguably the most
impressive in living memory. Ncube left the audience
in no doubt that Othello is the tragedy of a truly noble
hero. Especially memorable were the impression he gave
of appalled innocence and bewilderment in the face of
Iago's vision of corrupt sexuality, and both the intensity
of his suffering and the persistence of his love as he sinks
into barbarism.

Tom McAlindon.

Further Reading

The main source of the tragedy is included in *Eliʒabethan Love Stories*, ed. T. J. B. Spencer (1968), in Honigmann's Arden edition (1996) and (with other source material) in volume VIII of Geoffrey Bullough's *Narrative and Dramatic Sources of Shakespeare* (1973). Bullough examines Shakespeare's use of the source material, as does Kenneth Muir in his *The Sources of Shakespeare's Plays* (1977).

Editions with fuller commentary than the present one include the Cambridge (ed. Alice Walker and J. Dover Wilson, 1957), New Cambridge (ed. Norman Sanders, 1984) and the Arden (ed. E. A. J. Honigmann, 2001); also the *Complete Works*, ed. H. N. Hudson (1899). The best-known interpretation of the play is given in A. C. Bradley's *Shakespearean Tragedy* (1904). Its idealization of Othello has been faulted by numerous critics, most notably F. R. Leavis, who argued in his essay 'Diabolic Intellect and the Noble Hero' (in *The Common Pursuit*, 1952) that the hero's nobility is a disguise and that the tragedy was not caused by Iago but by Othello's self-deceiving and self-dramatizing egotism. Leavis was refuted by (among others) J. I. M. Stewart in *Character and Motive in Shakespeare* (1949), Helen Gardner in *The Noble Moor* (1956), Marvin Rosenberg in *The Masks of*

'*Othello*' (1961) and John Holloway in *The Story of the Night: Studies in Shakespeare's Major Tragedies* (1962); but his negative view of the Moor has been given new life in gender-oriented criticism such as Robin Headlam Wells's *Shakespeare on Masculinity* (2000), which reads the play as a critique of masculinist ideals and militaristic heroism.

R. B. Heilman's *Magic in the Web* (1956) studies the play as a series of interrelated contrasts or opposites. In another book-length study, '*Othello*' *as Tragedy: Some Problems of Judgement and Feeling* (1980), Jane Adamson seeks a response somewhere between Bradley and Leavis, one which includes recognition of Othello's culpability and 'feeling intensely for and with him'. Kenneth Muir's *Shakespeare's Tragic Sequence* (1979), Dieter Mehl's *Shakespeare's Tragedies: An Introduction* (1986) and John Russell Brown's *Shakespeare: The Tragedies* (2001) provide broad-based, chapter-length studies of the play (Brown's emphasizing performance). The chapters on *Othello* in Reuben Brower's *Hero and Saint: Shakespeare and the Graeco-Roman Heroic Tradition* (1971) and Robert Miola's *Shakespeare and Classical Tragedy* (1992) consider the play in the context of heroic tradition. Tom McAlindon's essay in *The Cambridge Companion to Shakespearean Tragedy*, ed. Claire McEachern (2003), 'What is a Shakespearean Tragedy?', provides a broad historical and generic context for the study of each of the tragedies and discusses the nature and significance of nobility in these plays. G. G. Sedgewick's *Of Irony: Especially in the Drama* (1935) has a chapter on the use of irony as preparation in *Othello*. The meanings assigned to the Mars–Venus myth during the Renaissance are discussed by Edgar Wind in his *Pagan Mysteries in the Renaissance* (2nd edn, 1967).

Three useful anthologies of critical essays are *Aspects of 'Othello'*, ed. Kenneth Muir and Philip Edwards (1977); the revised 1994 edition of the Macmillan Casebook, *Shakespeare: 'Othello'*, ed. John Wain; and *'Othello': New Perspectives*, ed. Virginia Mason Vaughan and Kent Cartwright (1991). Wain's collection reprints Bradley, Leavis and Gardner, as well as a feminist essay by Karen Newman. A notable feminist study in the Vaughan-Cartwright collection is Evelyn Gajowski's 'The Female Perspective in *Othello*'. The issue of race and colour is considered by George Hunter in his lecture 'Othello and Colour Prejudice', reprinted in his *Dramatic Identities and Cultural Tradition* (1978); by Ania Loomba in her *Gender, Race, Renaissance Drama* (1989) and *Shakespeare, Race and Colonialism* (2002); and by Virginia Mason Vaughan in *'Othello': A Contextual History* (1994). Barbara Everett's 'Inside *Othello*', in *Shakespeare Survey 53* (2000), deals with both race and gender. In 'Second Thoughts About *Othello*' (International Shakespeare Association Occasional Paper, 1999), the black British actor Hugh Quarshie argues that black actors should agree to act in this play only if it is made to show that Othello behaves as he does because he is a black man responding to racism.

The critical reception of the play is examined by Robert Hapgood in *Shakespeare: A Bibliographical Guide*, ed. Stanley Wells (1990), ch.11; by Peter Davison in *'Othello': An Introduction to the Variety of Criticism* (1988); and by Edward Pechter in his *'Othello' and Interpretive Traditions* (1999). Pechter seeks to describe *Othello*'s design and effects in a way that can account for its extraordinary power to engage the interests of audiences and readers, past and present.

Harley Granville Barker's *Prefaces to Shakespeare:*

'*Love's Labour's Lost*', '*Romeo and Juliet*', '*Merchant of Venice*', '*Othello*' (1958; illustrated edn, 1945) offers a performance-oriented study of the play and contains invaluable analyses of both the evolving action and the play's ambiguous time scheme. Studies of performance and performance history are Marvin Rosenberg's substantial *The Masks of 'Othello'*; Martin Wine's '*Othello': Text and Performance* (1984); Julie Hankey's *Plays in Performance: 'Othello'* (1987); Vaughan's '*Othello': A Contextual History*; and Lois Potter's *Shakespeare in Performance: 'Othello'* (2002). In *Players of Shakespeare 2*, ed. R. Jackson and R. Smallwood (1988), Ben Kingsley and David Suchet offer reflections on Othello and Iago (respectively) based on their experience of playing these parts in Terry Hands's RSC 1985 production.

THE TRAGEDY OF
OTHELLO,
THE MOOR OF VENICE

The Characters in the Play

OTHELLO, a Moor, General in the Venetian army
DESDEMONA, his wife
CASSIO, his Lieutenant
IAGO, his Ancient
EMILIA, wife of Iago
BIANCA, mistress of Cassio
RODERIGO, in love with Desdemona

The DUKE of Venice
BRABANTIO, a Venetian senator, Desdemona's father
GRATIANO, his brother
LODOVICO, his kinsman
MONTANO, Governor of Cyprus

SENATORS of Venice
OFFICERS
SAILOR
MESSENGER
GENTLEMEN of Cyprus
HERALD
A CLOWN in Othello's household
MUSICIANS

Soldiers, attendants, and servants

RODERIGO

   Tush, never tell me! I take it much unkindly

   That thou, Iago, who hast had my purse

   As if the strings were thine, shouldst know of this.

IAGO

   'Sblood, but you will not hear me!

   If ever I did dream of such a matter,

   Abhor me.

RODERIGO

   Thou told'st me thou didst hold him in thy hate.

IAGO

   Despise me, if I do not. Three great ones of the city,

   In personal suit to make me his Lieutenant,

   Off-capped to him: and by the faith of man,   10

   I know my price, I am worth no worse a place.

   But he, as loving his own pride and purposes,

   Evades them with a bombast circumstance

   Horribly stuffed with epithets of war,

   And in conclusion

   Non-suits my mediators. For 'Certes,' says he,

   'I have already chose my officer.'

   And what was he?

   Forsooth, a great arithmetician,

20   One Michael Cassio, a Florentine –
       A fellow almost damned in a fair wife –
       That never set a squadron in the field,
       Nor the division of a battle knows
       More than a spinster – unless the bookish theoric,
       Wherein the togèd consuls can propose
       As masterly as he. Mere prattle without practice
       Is all his soldiership. But he, sir, had th'election:
       And I, of whom his eyes had seen the proof
       At Rhodes, at Cyprus, and on other grounds
30   Christian and heathen, must be leed and calmed
       By debitor and creditor; this counter-caster,
       He in good time must his Lieutenant be,
       And I – God bless the mark! – his Moorship's Ancient.
RODERIGO
       By heaven, I rather would have been his hangman.
IAGO
       Why, there's no remedy. 'Tis the curse of service:
       Preferment goes by letter and affection,
       And not by old gradation, where each second
       Stood heir to th'first. Now sir, be judge yourself
       Whether I in any just term am affined
40   To love the Moor.
RODERIGO
       I would not follow him then.
IAGO   O, sir, content you:
       I follow him to serve my turn upon him.
       We cannot all be masters, nor all masters
       Cannot be truly followed. You shall mark
       Many a duteous and knee-crooking knave
       That, doting on his own obsequious bondage,
       Wears out his time, much like his master's ass,
       For naught but provender, and when he's old – cashiered!
       Whip me such honest knaves. Others there are

Who, trimmed in forms and visages of duty,   50
Keep yet their hearts attending on themselves,
And, throwing but shows of service on their lords,
Do well thrive by them; and when they have lined their
     coats,
Do themselves homage: these fellows have some soul,
And such a one do I profess myself.
For, sir,
It is as sure as you are Roderigo,
Were I the Moor, I would not be Iago:
In following him, I follow but myself.
Heaven is my judge, not I for love and duty,   60
But seeming so for my peculiar end:
For when my outward action doth demonstrate
The native act and figure of my heart
In compliment extern, 'tis not long after,
But I will wear my heart upon my sleeve
For daws to peck at – I am not what I am.

RODERIGO

What a full fortune does the thick-lips owe
If he can carry't thus!

IAGO   Call up her father,
Rouse him, make after him, poison his delight,
Proclaim him in the streets; incense her kinsmen,   70
And, though he in a fertile climate dwell,
Plague him with flies: though that his joy be joy,
Yet throw such chances of vexation on't,
As it may lose some colour.

RODERIGO

Here is her father's house; I'll call aloud.

IAGO

Do, with like timorous accent and dire yell,
As when, by night and negligence, the fire
Is spied in populous cities.

RODERIGO

What, ho, Brabantio! Signor Brabantio, ho!

IAGO

80   Awake! What, ho, Brabantio! Thieves, thieves!
Look to your house, your daughter, and your bags!
Thieves, thieves!

Enter Brabantio above, at a window

BRABANTIO

What is the reason of this terrible summons?
What is the matter there?

RODERIGO

Signor, is all your family within?

IAGO

Are your doors locked?

BRABANTIO   Why, wherefore ask you this?

IAGO

Zounds, sir, you're robbed; for shame, put on your gown;
Your heart is burst, you have lost half your soul.
Even now, now, very now, an old black ram

90   Is tupping your white ewe. Arise, arise,
Awake the snorting citizens with the bell,
Or else the devil will make a grandsire of you.
Arise, I say!

BRABANTIO   What, have you lost your wits?

RODERIGO

Most reverend signor, do you know my voice?

BRABANTIO

Not I: what are you?

RODERIGO   My name is Roderigo.

BRABANTIO

The worser welcome!
I have charged thee not to haunt about my doors.
In honest plainness thou hast heard me say
My daughter is not for thee. And now in madness,

Being full of supper and distempering draughts,   100
Upon malicious bravery dost thou come
To start my quiet.

RODERIGO
Sir, sir, sir –

BRABANTIO   But thou must needs be sure
My spirit and my place have in them power
To make this bitter to thee.

RODERIGO   Patience, good sir.

BRABANTIO
What tell'st thou me of robbing? This is Venice:
My house is not a grange.

RODERIGO   Most grave Brabantio,
In simple and pure soul I come to you . . .

IAGO Zounds, sir, you are one of those that will not serve
God if the devil bid you. Because we come to do you   110
service, and you think we are ruffians, you'll have your
daughter covered with a Barbary horse; you'll have your
nephews neigh to you, you'll have coursers for cousins,
and jennets for germans.

BRABANTIO What profane wretch art thou?

IAGO I am one, sir, that comes to tell you, your daughter
and the Moor are now making the beast with two
backs.

BRABANTIO
Thou art a villain.

IAGO   You are a Senator.

BRABANTIO
This thou shalt answer. I know thee, Roderigo.   120

RODERIGO
Sir, I will answer anything. But I beseech you
If 't be your pleasure and most wise consent,
As partly I find it is, that your fair daughter,
At this odd-even and dull watch o'th'night,

Transported with no worse nor better guard
But with a knave of common hire, a gondolier,
To the gross clasps of a lascivious Moor –
If this be known to you, and your allowance,
We then have done you bold and saucy wrongs;
130   But if you know not this, my manners tell me
We have your wrong rebuke. Do not believe
That from the sense of all civility
I thus would play and trifle with your reverence.
Your daughter, if you have not given her leave,
I say again hath made a gross revolt,
Tying her duty, beauty, wit, and fortunes
In an extravagant and wheeling stranger
Of here and everywhere. Straight satisfy yourself:
If she be in her chamber or your house,
140   Let loose on me the justice of the state
For thus deluding you.

BRABANTIO   Strike on the tinder, ho!
Give me a taper; call up all my people!
This accident is not unlike my dream:
Belief of it oppresses me already.
Light, I say, light!   *Exit above*

IAGO   Farewell, for I must leave you.
It seems not meet, nor wholesome to my place,
To be produced – as if I stay, I shall –
Against the Moor. For I do know the state,
However this may gall him with some check,
150   Cannot with safety cast him; for he's embarked
With such loud reason to the Cyprus wars,
Which even now stand in act, that for their souls
Another of his fathom they have none
To lead their business. In which regard,
Though I do hate him as I do hell pains,
Yet for necessity of present life

I must show out a flag and sign of love,
Which is indeed but sign. That you shall surely find him,
Lead to the Sagittary the raisèd search;
And there will I be with him. So farewell.   *Exit*   160
   Enter Brabantio in his night-gown with servants and
   torches

BRABANTIO
It is too true an evil. Gone she is,
And what's to come of my despisèd time
Is naught but bitterness. Now, Roderigo,
Where didst thou see her? – O unhappy girl! –
With the Moor, say'st thou? – Who would be a father? –
How didst thou know 'twas she? – O, she deceives me
Past thought! – What said she to you? – Get more tapers.
Raise all my kindred. – Are they married, think you?

RODERIGO
Truly I think they are.

BRABANTIO
O heaven! How got she out? O treason of the blood!   170
Fathers, from hence trust not your daughters' minds
By what you see them act. Is there not charms
By which the property of youth and maidhood
May be abused? Have you not read, Roderigo,
Of some such thing?

RODERIGO   Yes, sir, I have indeed.

BRABANTIO
Call up my brother – O would you had had her!
Some one way, some another. Do you know
Where we may apprehend her and the Moor?

RODERIGO
I think I can discover him, if you please
To get good guard and go along with me.   180

BRABANTIO
Pray you, lead on. At every house I'll call –

I may command at most. Get weapons, ho!
And raise some special officers of night.
On, good Roderigo, I'll deserve your pains.   *Exeunt*

I.2   *Enter Othello, Iago, attendants with torches*

IAGO
Though in the trade of war I have slain men,
Yet do I hold it very stuff o'th'conscience
To do no contrived murder: I lack iniquity
Sometimes to do me service. Nine or ten times
I had thought t'have yerked him here under the ribs.

OTHELLO
'Tis better as it is.

IAGO   Nay, but he prated
And spoke such scurvy and provoking terms
Against your honour,
That with the little godliness I have,
10   I did full hard forbear him. But I pray, sir,
Are you fast married? For be assured of this,
That the Magnifico is much beloved,
And hath in his effect a voice potential
As double as the Duke's. He will divorce you,
Or put upon you what restraint and grievance
That law, with all his might to enforce it on,
Will give him cable.

OTHELLO   Let him do his spite:
My services, which I have done the signory,
Shall out-tongue his complaints. 'Tis yet to know –
20   Which, when I know that boasting is an honour,
I shall provulgate – I fetch my life and being
From men of royal siege, and my demerits
May speak, unbonneted, to as proud a fortune
As this that I have reached. For know, Iago,

But that I love the gentle Desdemona,
I would not my unhousèd free condition
Put into circumscription and confine
For the seas' worth. But look, what lights come yond!

IAGO

Those are the raisèd father and his friends:
You were best go in.

OTHELLO   Not I: I must be found.   30
My parts, my title, and my perfect soul
Shall manifest me rightly. Is it they?

IAGO

By Janus, I think no.
        Enter Cassio, with men bearing torches

OTHELLO

The servants of the Duke and my Lieutenant!
The goodness of the night upon you, friends.
What is the news?

CASSIO   The Duke does greet you, General,
And he requires your haste-post-haste appearance
Even on the instant.

OTHELLO   What is the matter, think you?

CASSIO

Something from Cyprus, as I may divine:
It is a business of some heat. The galleys   40
Have sent a dozen sequent messengers
This very night at one another's heels;
And many of the consuls, raised and met,
Are at the Duke's already. You have been hotly called for,
When being not at your lodging to be found.
The senate hath sent about three several quests
To search you out.

OTHELLO   'Tis well I am found by you:
I will but spend a word here in the house
And go with you.   *Exit*

CASSIO   Ancient, what makes he here?
IAGO
50 Faith, he tonight hath boarded a land carack:
    If it prove lawful prize, he's made for ever.
CASSIO
    I do not understand.
IAGO   He's married.
CASSIO   To who?
IAGO
    Marry, to – Come, Captain, will you go?
        Enter Othello
OTHELLO   Have with you.
CASSIO
    Here comes another troop to seek for you.
        Enter Brabantio, Roderigo, with Officers and torches
IAGO
    It is Brabantio: General, be advised,
    He comes to bad intent.
OTHELLO   Holla, stand there.
RODERIGO
    Signor, it is the Moor.
BRABANTIO   Down with him, thief!
IAGO
    You, Roderigo? Come, sir, I am for you.
OTHELLO
    Keep up your bright swords, for the dew will rust them.
60 Good signor, you shall more command with years
    Than with your weapons.
BRABANTIO
    O thou foul thief! Where hast thou stowed my daughter?
    Damned as thou art, thou hast enchanted her:
    For I'll refer me to all things of sense,
    If she in chains of magic were not bound,
    Whether a maid, so tender, fair, and happy,

So opposite to marriage that she shunned
The wealthy curlèd darlings of our nation,
Would ever have – t'incur a general mock –
Run from her guardage to the sooty bosom   70
Of such a thing as thou: to fear, not to delight.
Judge me the world, if 'tis not gross in sense
That thou hast practised on her with foul charms,
Abused her delicate youth with drugs or minerals
That weakens motion. I'll have't disputed on;
'Tis probable, and palpable to thinking:
I therefore apprehend, and do attach thee
For an abuser of the world, a practiser
Of arts inhibited, and out of warrant.
Lay hold upon him: if he do resist,   80
Subdue him, at his peril.

OTHELLO   Hold your hands,
Both you of my inclining and the rest.
Were it my cue to fight, I should have known it
Without a prompter. Where will you that I go
To answer this your charge?

BRABANTIO   To prison, till fit time
Of law and course of direct session
Call thee to answer.

OTHELLO   What if I do obey?
How may the Duke be therewith satisfied,
Whose messengers are here about my side,
Upon some present business of the state   90
To bring me to him?

OFFICER   'Tis true, most worthy signor:
The Duke's in council, and your noble self
I am sure is sent for.

BRABANTIO   How? The Duke in council?
In this time of the night? Bring him away.
Mine's not an idle cause; the Duke himself,

Or any of my brothers of the state,
Cannot but feel this wrong as 'twere their own:
For if such actions may have passage free,
Bondslaves and pagans shall our statesmen be.   *Exeunt*

I.3   *The Duke and Senators sitting at a table; with lights*
            and attendants

DUKE
    There is no composition in these news
    That gives them credit.

FIRST SENATOR   Indeed they are disproportioned.
    My letters say a hundred and seven galleys.

DUKE
    And mine, a hundred and forty.

SECOND SENATOR   And mine two hundred;
    But though they jump not on a just accompt –
    As in these cases where the aim reports
    'Tis oft with difference – yet do they all confirm
    A Turkish fleet, and bearing up to Cyprus.

DUKE
    Nay, it is possible enough to judgement:
10   I do not so secure me in the error,
    But the main article I do approve
    In fearful sense.

SAILOR (*without*) What, ho! What, ho! What, ho!

FIRST OFFICER
    A messenger from the galleys.
        Enter Sailor

DUKE   Now, what's the business?

SAILOR
    The Turkish preparation makes for Rhodes;
    So was I bid report here to the state
    By Signor Angelo.

DUKE
  How say you by this change?
FIRST SENATOR   This cannot be,
  By no assay of reason. 'Tis a pageant
  To keep us in false gaze. When we consider
  Th'importancy of Cyprus to the Turk,   20
  And let ourselves again but understand
  That as it more concerns the Turk than Rhodes,
  So may he with more facile question bear it,
  For that it stands not in such warlike brace,
  But altogether lacks th'abilities
  That Rhodes is dressed in. If we make thought of this,
  We must not think the Turk is so unskilful
  To leave that latest which concerns him first,
  Neglecting an attempt of ease and gain
  To wake and wage a danger profitless.   30
DUKE
  Nay, in all confidence he's not for Rhodes.
FIRST OFFICER
  Here is more news.
      Enter a Messenger
MESSENGER
  The Ottomites, reverend and gracious,
  Steering with due course toward the isle of Rhodes,
  Have there injointed with an after fleet.
FIRST SENATOR
  Ay, so I thought. How many, as you guess?
MESSENGER
  Of thirty sail; and now they do re-stem
  Their backward course, bearing with frank appearance
  Their purposes toward Cyprus. Signor Montano,
  Your trusty and most valiant servitor,   40
  With his free duty recommends you thus,
  And prays you to believe him.

DUKE
      'Tis certain then for Cyprus.
      Marcus Luccicos, is not he in town?
FIRST SENATOR
      He's now in Florence.
DUKE   Write from us: wish him
      Post-post-haste dispatch.
FIRST SENATOR
      Here comes Brabantio and the valiant Moor.
            Enter Brabantio, Othello, Iago, Roderigo, and Officers
DUKE
      Valiant Othello, we must straight employ you
      Against the general enemy Ottoman.
50   (*To Brabantio*) I did not see you: welcome, gentle
            signor;
      We lacked your counsel and your help tonight.
BRABANTIO
      So did I yours. Good your grace, pardon me:
      Neither my place, nor aught I heard of business,
      Hath raised me from my bed; nor doth the general care
      Take hold on me; for my particular grief
      Is of so flood-gate and o'erbearing nature
      That it engluts and swallows other sorrows
      And yet is still itself.
DUKE   Why? What's the matter?
BRABANTIO
      My daughter! O, my daughter!
SENATORS   Dead?
BRABANTIO   Ay, to me.
60   She is abused, stolen from me, and corrupted
      By spells and medicines bought of mountebanks;
      For nature so preposterously to err,
      Being not deficient, blind, or lame of sense,
      Sans witchcraft could not.

DUKE

>Whoe'er he be that in this foul proceeding
>Hath thus beguiled your daughter of herself
>And you of her, the bloody book of law
>You shall yourself read in the bitter letter
>After your own sense, yea, though our proper son
>Stood in your action.

BRABANTIO   Humbly I thank your grace.   70

>Here is the man: this Moor, whom now it seems
>Your special mandate for the state affairs
>Hath hither brought.

ALL   We are very sorry for't.

DUKE

>What in your own part can you say to this?

BRABANTIO

>Nothing, but this is so.

OTHELLO

>Most potent, grave and reverend signors,
>My very noble and approved good masters,
>That I have ta'en away this old man's daughter,
>It is most true; true I have married her;
>The very head and front of my offending   80
>Hath this extent, no more. Rude am I in my speech
>And little blessed with the soft phrase of peace;
>For since these arms of mine had seven years' pith
>Till now some nine moons wasted, they have used
>Their dearest action in the tented field;
>And little of this great world can I speak
>More than pertains to feats of broil and battle;
>And therefore little shall I grace my cause
>In speaking for myself. Yet, by your gracious patience,
>I will a round unvarnished tale deliver   90
>Of my whole course of love: what drugs, what charms,
>What conjuration and what mighty magic –

For such proceedings I am charged withal –
I won his daughter.

BRABANTIO   A maiden never bold;
Of spirit so still and quiet that her motion
Blushed at herself: and she, in spite of nature,
Of years, of country, credit, everything,
To fall in love with what she feared to look on!
It is a judgement maimed and most imperfect
That will confess perfection so could err
Against all rules of nature, and must be driven
To find out practices of cunning hell
Why this should be. I therefore vouch again
That with some mixtures powerful o'er the blood,
Or with some dram conjured to this effect,
He wrought upon her.

DUKE   To vouch this is no proof,
Without more wider and more overt test
Than these thin habits and poor likelihoods
Of modern seeming do prefer against him.

FIRST SENATOR
But, Othello, speak:
Did you by indirect and forcèd courses
Subdue and poison this young maid's affections?
Or came it by request and such fair question
As soul to soul affordeth?

OTHELLO   I do beseech you,
Send for the lady to the Sagittary,
And let her speak of me before her father.
If you do find me foul in her report,
The trust, the office I do hold of you
Not only take away, but let your sentence
Even fall upon my life.

DUKE   Fetch Desdemona hither.

OTHELLO
    Ancient, conduct them: you best know the place.

                Exit Iago with attendants

    And till she come, as truly as to heaven
    I do confess the vices of my blood,
    So justly to your grave ears I'll present
    How I did thrive in this fair lady's love,
    And she in mine.

DUKE   Say it, Othello.

OTHELLO
    Her father loved me, oft invited me,
    Still questioned me the story of my life
    From year to year – the battles, sieges, fortunes
    That I have passed.   130
    I ran it through, even from my boyish days
    To th'very moment that he bade me tell it:
    Wherein I spake of most disastrous chances,
    Of moving accidents by flood and field,
    Of hair-breadth scapes i'th'imminent deadly breach,
    Of being taken by the insolent foe,
    And sold to slavery; of my redemption thence,
    And portance in my travels' history:
    Wherein of antres vast and deserts idle,
    Rough quarries, rocks, and hills whose heads touch
        heaven,   140
    It was my hint to speak – such was the process:
    And of the Cannibals that each other eat,
    The Anthropophagi, and men whose heads
    Do grow beneath their shoulders. This to hear
    Would Desdemona seriously incline:
    But still the house affairs would draw her thence,
    Which ever as she could with haste dispatch
    She'd come again, and with a greedy ear
    Devour up my discourse; which I observing

150   Took once a pliant hour, and found good means
    To draw from her a prayer of earnest heart
    That I would all my pilgrimage dilate
    Whereof by parcels she had something heard,
    But not intentively. I did consent,
    And often did beguile her of her tears
    When I did speak of some distressful stroke
    That my youth suffered. My story being done,
    She gave me for my pains a world of sighs:
    She swore, in faith 'twas strange, 'twas passing strange,
160   'Twas pitiful, 'twas wondrous pitiful;
    She wished she had not heard it, yet she wished
    That heaven had made her such a man. She thanked me,
    And bade me, if I had a friend that loved her,
    I should but teach him how to tell my story,
    And that would woo her. Upon this hint I spake:
    She loved me for the dangers I had passed,
    And I loved her, that she did pity them.
    This only is the witchcraft I have used.
    Here comes the lady: let her witness it.
       Enter Desdemona, Iago, and attendants

DUKE
170   I think this tale would win my daughter too.
    Good Brabantio, take up this mangled matter at the best:
    Men do their broken weapons rather use
    Than their bare hands.

BRABANTIO   I pray you hear her speak.
    If she confess that she was half the wooer,
    Destruction on my head, if my bad blame
    Light on the man! Come hither, gentle mistress;
    Do you perceive in all this company
    Where most you owe obedience?

DESDEMONA   My noble father,
    I do perceive here a divided duty:

To you I am bound for life and education;   180
My life and education both do learn me
How to respect you. You are lord of all my duty,
I am hitherto your daughter. But here's my husband;
And so much duty as my mother showed
To you, preferring you before her father,
So much I challenge, that I may profess
Due to the Moor, my lord.
BRABANTIO   God bu'y! I have done.
Please it your grace, on to the state affairs.
I had rather to adopt a child than get it.
Come hither, Moor: 190
I here do give thee that with all my heart
Which, but thou hast already, with all my heart
I would keep from thee. For your sake, jewel,
I am glad at soul I have no other child,
For thy escape would teach me tyranny
To hang clogs on them. I have done, my lord.
DUKE
Let me speak like yourself and lay a sentence
Which as a grise or step may help these lovers
Into your favour.
When remedies are past the griefs are ended   200
By seeing the worst which late on hopes depended.
To mourn a mischief that is past and gone
Is the next way to draw new mischief on.
What cannot be preserved when fortune takes,
Patience her injury a mockery makes.
The robbed that smiles steals something from the thief;
He robs himself that spends a bootless grief.
BRABANTIO
So let the Turk of Cyprus us beguile,
We lose it not so long as we can smile;
He bears the sentence well that nothing bears   210

But the free comfort which from thence he hears;
But he bears both the sentence and the sorrow
That to pay grief must of poor patience borrow.
These sentences, to sugar or to gall
Being strong on both sides, are equivocal.
But words are words; I never yet did hear
That the bruised heart was piecèd through the ear.
I humbly beseech you proceed to th'affairs of state.

DUKE The Turk with a most mighty preparation makes for
220   Cyprus. Othello, the fortitude of the place is best known
to you: and though we have there a substitute of most
allowed sufficiency, yet opinion, a more sovereign mistress of effects, throws a more safer voice on you. You
must therefore be content to slubber the gloss of your
new fortunes with this more stubborn and boisterous
expedition.

OTHELLO
The tyrant, custom, most grave Senators,
Hath made the flinty and steel couch of war
My thrice-driven bed of down. I do agnize
230   A natural and prompt alacrity
I find in hardness; and do undertake
This present war against the Ottomites.
Most humbly, therefore, bending to your state,
I crave fit disposition for my wife,
Due reference of place and exhibition,
With such accommodation and besort
As levels with her breeding.

DUKE   If you please,
Be't at her father's.

BRABANTIO   I'll not have it so.

OTHELLO
Nor I.

DESDEMONA Nor I: I would not there reside

To put my father in impatient thoughts   240
By being in his eye. Most gracious Duke,
To my unfolding lend your prosperous ear,
And let me find a charter in your voice
T'assist my simpleness.
DUKE   What would you? Speak.
DESDEMONA
   That I did love the Moor to live with him,
My downright violence and storm of fortunes
May trumpet to the world. My heart's subdued
Even to the very quality of my lord.
I saw Othello's visage in his mind
And to his honours and his valiant parts   250
Did I my soul and fortunes consecrate.
So that, dear lords, if I be left behind
A moth of peace, and he go to the war,
The rites for which I love him are bereft me,
And I a heavy interim shall support
By his dear absence. Let me go with him.
OTHELLO
   Let her have your voice.
Vouch with me, heaven, I therefore beg it not
To please the palate of my appetite,
Nor to comply with heat – the young affects   260
In me defunct – and proper satisfaction;
But to be free and bounteous to her mind.
And heaven defend your good souls that you think
I will your serious and great business scant
For she is with me. No, when light-winged toys
Of feathered Cupid seel with wanton dullness
My speculative and officed instruments,
That my disports corrupt and taint my business,
Let housewives make a skillet of my helm,
And all indign and base adversities   270
Make head against my estimation!

DUKE

    Be it as you shall privately determine,

    Either for her stay, or going. Th'affair cries haste,

    And speed must answer it. You must hence tonight.

DESDEMONA

    Tonight, my lord?

DUKE   This night.

OTHELLO   With all my heart.

DUKE

    At nine i'th'morning, here we'll meet again.

    Othello, leave some officer behind,

    And he shall our commission bring to you,

    With such things else of quality and respect

280   As doth import you.

OTHELLO   So please your grace, my Ancient.

    A man he is of honesty and trust:

    To his conveyance I assign my wife,

    With what else needful your good grace shall think

    To be sent after me.

DUKE   Let it be so.

    Good night to everyone. And, noble signor,

    If virtue no delighted beauty lack,

    Your son-in-law is far more fair than black.

FIRST SENATOR

    Adieu, brave Moor: use Desdemona well.

BRABANTIO

    Look to her, Moor, if thou hast eyes to see.

290   She has deceived her father, and may thee.

OTHELLO

    My life upon her faith!

              Exeunt Duke, Senators, and attendants

              Honest Iago,

    My Desdemona must I leave to thee.

    I prithee let thy wife attend on her,

And bring them after in the best advantage.
Come, Desdemona, I have but an hour
Of love, of worldly matters and direction
To spend with thee. We must obey the time.

Exeunt Othello and Desdemona

RODERIGO Iago.

IAGO What say'st thou, noble heart?

RODERIGO What will I do, think'st thou?   300

IAGO Why, go to bed and sleep.

RODERIGO I will incontinently drown myself.

IAGO If thou dost, I shall never love thee after. Why, thou
silly gentleman!

RODERIGO It is silliness to live, when to live is torment:
and then we have a prescription to die, when death is
our physician.

IAGO O villainous! I have looked upon the world for four
times seven years, and since I could distinguish betwixt
a benefit and an injury, I never found a man that knew   310
how to love himself. Ere I would say I would drown
myself for the love of a guinea-hen, I would change my
humanity with a baboon.

RODERIGO What should I do? I confess it is my shame to
be so fond, but it is not in my virtue to amend it.

IAGO Virtue? A fig! 'Tis in ourselves that we are thus, or
thus. Our bodies are our gardens, to the which our wills
are gardeners. So that if we will plant nettles or sow
lettuce, set hyssop and weed up thyme, supply it with
one gender of herbs or distract it with many, either to   320
have it sterile with idleness or manured with industry,
why the power and corrigible authority of this lies
in our wills. If the beam of our lives had not one scale
of reason to poise another of sensuality, the blood and
baseness of our natures would conduct us to most
preposterous conclusions. But we have reason to cool

our raging motions, our carnal stings, our unbitted lusts:
whereof I take this, that you call love, to be a sect or
scion.

330 RODERIGO It cannot be.

IAGO It is merely a lust of the blood and a permission of
the will. Come, be a man. Drown thyself? Drown cats
and blind puppies. I have professed me thy friend, and
I confess me knit to thy deserving with cables of perdurable toughness. I could never better stead thee than
now. Put money in thy purse. Follow thou these wars;
defeat thy favour with an usurped beard. I say, put
money in thy purse. It cannot be that Desdemona should
long continue her love to the Moor – put money in thy
340 purse – nor he his to her. It was a violent commence-
ment, and thou shalt see an answerable sequestration –
put but money in thy purse. These Moors are change-
able in their wills – fill thy purse with money. The food
that to him now is as luscious as locusts shall be to him
shortly as acerbe as the coloquintida. She must change
for youth: when she is sated with his body she will find
the error of her choice. Therefore put money in thy
purse. If thou wilt needs damn thyself, do it a more
delicate way than drowning. Make all the money thou
350 canst. If sanctimony and a frail vow betwixt an erring
barbarian and a super-subtle Venetian be not too hard
for my wits and all the tribe of hell, thou shalt enjoy
her – therefore make money. A pox of drowning thyself!
It is clean out of the way. Seek thou rather to be hanged
in compassing thy joy than to be drowned and go without her.

RODERIGO Wilt thou be fast to my hopes, if I depend on
the issue?

IAGO Thou art sure of me. Go make money. I have told
360 thee often, and I re-tell thee again and again, I hate

the Moor. My cause is hearted: thine hath no less
reason. Let us be conjunctive in our revenge against
him. If thou canst cuckold him, thou dost thyself a
pleasure, me a sport. There are many events in the
womb of time, which will be delivered. Traverse! Go,
provide thy money. We will have more of this tomorrow.
Adieu.

RODERIGO Where shall we meet i'th'morning?

IAGO At my lodging.

RODERIGO I'll be with thee betimes.   370

IAGO Go to; farewell. Do you hear, Roderigo?

RODERIGO What say you?

IAGO No more of drowning, do you hear?

RODERIGO I am changed.

IAGO Go to; farewell. Put money enough in your purse.

RODERIGO I'll sell all my land.   *Exit*

IAGO

    Thus do I ever make my fool my purse:
    For I mine own gained knowledge should profane
    If I would time expend with such a snipe
    But for my sport and profit. I hate the Moor,   380
    And it is thought abroad that 'twixt my sheets
    He's done my office. I know not if 't be true
    But I, for mere suspicion in that kind,
    Will do as if for surety. He holds me well:
    The better shall my purpose work on him.
    Cassio's a proper man: let me see now;
    To get his place and to plume up my will
    In double knavery. How? How? Let's see.
    After some time, to abuse Othello's ear
    That he is too familiar with his wife;   390
    He hath a person and a smooth dispose
    To be suspected, framed to make women false.
    The Moor is of a free and open nature,

That thinks men honest that but seem to be so,
And will as tenderly be led by th'nose
As asses are.
I have't. It is engendered. Hell and night
Must bring this monstrous birth to the world's light.

                                                    Exit

                              *

II.1   *Enter Montano and two Gentlemen*
MONTANO
    What from the cape can you discern at sea?
FIRST GENTLEMAN
    Nothing at all; it is a high-wrought flood.
    I cannot 'twixt the heaven and the main
    Descry a sail.
MONTANO
    Methinks the wind does speak aloud at land;
    A fuller blast ne'er shook our battlements.
    If it hath ruffianed so upon the sea,
    What ribs of oak, when mountains melt on them,
    Can hold the mortise? What shall we hear of this?
SECOND GENTLEMAN
10 A segregation of the Turkish fleet:
    For do but stand upon the banning shore,
    The chidden billow seems to pelt the clouds;
    The wind-shaked surge, with high and monstrous mane,
    Seems to cast water on the burning Bear
    And quench the guards of th'ever-fixèd Pole.
    I never did like molestation view
    On the enchafèd flood.
MONTANO   If that the Turkish fleet
    Be not ensheltered and embayed, they are drowned:

It is impossible they bear it out.

Enter a Gentleman

THIRD GENTLEMAN

News, lads! Our wars are done: 20
The desperate tempest hath so banged the Turks
That their designment halts. A noble ship of Venice
Hath seen a grievous wrack and sufferance
On most part of their fleet.

MONTANO

How! Is this true?

THIRD GENTLEMAN The ship is here put in,
A Veronesa; Michael Cassio,
Lieutenant to the warlike Moor, Othello,
Is come on shore; the Moor himself at sea,
And is in full commission here for Cyprus.

MONTANO

I am glad on't; 'tis a worthy governor.   30

THIRD GENTLEMAN

But this same Cassio, though he speak of comfort
Touching the Turkish loss, yet he looks sadly
And prays the Moor be safe; for they were parted
With foul and violent tempest.

MONTANO   Pray heaven he be:
For I have served him, and the man commands
Like a full soldier. Let's to the sea-side, ho!
As well to see the vessel that's come in,
As to throw out our eyes for brave Othello,
Even till we make the main and th'aerial blue
An indistinct regard.

THIRD GENTLEMAN   Come, let's do so;   40
For every minute is expectancy
Of more arrivance.

Enter Cassio

CASSIO

    Thanks, you the valiant of this warlike isle
    That so approve the Moor! O, let the heavens
    Give him defence against the elements,
    For I have lost him on a dangerous sea.

MONTANO

    Is he well shipped?

CASSIO

    His bark is stoutly timbered, and his pilot
    Of very expert and approved allowance;
50   Therefore my hopes, not surfeited to death,
    Stand in bold cure.
        (*Cry within*) 'A sail, a sail, a sail!'

CASSIO

    What noise?

GENTLEMAN

    The town is empty; on the brow o'th'sea
    Stand ranks of people, and they cry 'A sail!'

CASSIO

    My hopes do shape him for the Governor.
    Salvo

SECOND GENTLEMAN

    They do discharge their shot of courtesy:
    Our friends at least.

CASSIO   I pray you, sir, go forth,
    And give us truth who 'tis that is arrived.

SECOND GENTLEMAN

    I shall.   *Exit*

MONTANO

60   But, good Lieutenant, is your General wived?

CASSIO

    Most fortunately: he hath achieved a maid
    That paragons description and wild fame;
    One that excels the quirks of blazoning pens,

And in th'essential vesture of creation
Does tire the ingener.
>   *Enter Second Gentleman*
>   How now? Who has put in?

SECOND GENTLEMAN
'Tis one Iago, Ancient to the General.

CASSIO
He's had most favourable and happy speed:
Tempests themselves, high seas, and howling winds,
The guttered rocks and congregated sands,
Traitors enscarped to clog the guiltless keel,   70
As having sense of beauty, do omit
Their mortal natures, letting go safely by
The divine Desdemona.

MONTANO   What is she?

CASSIO
She that I spake of, our great Captain's Captain,
Left in the conduct of the bold Iago,
Whose footing here anticipates our thoughts
A se'nnight's speed. Great Jove, Othello guard,
And swell his sail with thine own powerful breath,
That he may bless this bay with his tall ship,
Make love's quick pants in Desdemona's arms,   80
Give renewed fire to our extinced spirits,
And bring all Cyprus comfort.
>   *Enter Desdemona, Emilia, Iago, Roderigo, and*
>   *attendants*
>   O, behold,
The riches of the ship is come on shore!
You men of Cyprus, let her have your knees.
Hail to thee, lady! And the grace of heaven,
Before, behind thee, and on every hand,
Enwheel thee round.

DESDEMONA   I thank you, valiant Cassio.

What tidings can you tell me of my lord?

CASSIO

He is not yet arrived; nor know I aught
90   But that he's well, and will be shortly here.

DESDEMONA

O, but I fear! How lost you company?

CASSIO

The great contention of the sea and skies
Parted our fellowship.
                    (*Cry within*) 'A sail, a sail!'
                                              But hark, a sail!

GENTLEMAN

They give their greeting to the citadel:
This likewise is a friend.

CASSIO   See for the news.
Good Ancient, you are welcome. Welcome, mistress.
Let it not gall your patience, good Iago,
That I extend my manners. 'Tis my breeding
That gives me this bold show of courtesy.
       He kisses Emilia

IAGO

100   Sir, would she give you so much of her lips
As of her tongue she oft bestows on me,
You'd have enough.

DESDEMONA

Alas, she has no speech.

IAGO   In faith, too much.
I find it still when I have list to sleep.
Marry, before your ladyship, I grant
She puts her tongue a little in her heart
And chides with thinking.

EMILIA   You have little cause to say so.

IAGO Come on, come on: you are pictures out of doors,
bells in your parlours, wild-cats in your kitchens, saints

in your injuries, devils being offended, players in your   110
housewifery, and housewives in your beds.

DESDEMONA

O, fie upon thee, slanderer!

IAGO

Nay, it is true, or else I am a Turk:
You rise to play and go to bed to work.

EMILIA

You shall not write my praise.

IAGO   No, let me not.

DESDEMONA

What wouldst thou write of me, if thou shouldst praise
      me?

IAGO

O, gentle lady, do not put me to't,
For I am nothing if not critical.

DESDEMONA

Come on, assay. There's one gone to the harbour?

IAGO

Ay, madam.   120

DESDEMONA

(aside) I am not merry, but I do beguile
The thing I am by seeming otherwise.
Come, how wouldst thou praise me?

IAGO

I am about it, but indeed my invention
Comes from my pate as birdlime does from frieze –
It plucks out brains and all. But my muse labours,
And thus she is delivered.
If she be fair and wise, fairness and wit,
The one's for use, the other useth it.

DESDEMONA

Well praised! How if she be black and witty?   130

IAGO

    If she be black, and thereto have a wit,

    She'll find a white that shall her blackness fit.

DESDEMONA

    Worse and worse.

EMILIA   How if fair and foolish?

IAGO

    She never yet was foolish that was fair,

    For even her folly helped her to an heir.

DESDEMONA These are old fond paradoxes to make fools

    laugh i'th'alehouse. What miserable praise hast thou for

    her that's foul and foolish?

IAGO

    There's none so foul and foolish thereunto,

140   But does foul pranks which fair and wise ones do.

DESDEMONA O heavy ignorance! Thou praisest the worst

    best. But what praise couldst thou bestow on a deserving

    woman indeed? One that in the authority of her merit

    did justly put on the vouch of very malice itself?

IAGO

    She that was ever fair and never proud,

    Had tongue at will, and yet was never loud;

    Never lacked gold, and yet went never gay;

    Fled from her wish, and yet said 'Now I may';

    She that being angered, her revenge being nigh,

150   Bade her wrong stay, and her displeasure fly;

    She that in wisdom never was so frail

    To change the cod's head for the salmon's tail;

    She that could think and ne'er disclose her mind:

    See suitors following and not look behind:

    She was a wight, if ever such wight were –

DESDEMONA

    To do what?

IAGO
   To suckle fools and chronicle small beer.
DESDEMONA
   O, most lame and impotent conclusion!
   Do not learn of him, Emilia, though he be thy husband.
   How say you, Cassio, is he not a most profane and   160
   liberal counsellor?
CASSIO He speaks home, madam; you may relish him more
   in the soldier than in the scholar.
IAGO (*aside*) He takes her by the palm. Ay, well said,
   whisper. With as little a web as this will I ensnare as
   great a fly as Cassio. Ay, smile upon her, do. I will
   gyve thee in thine own courtship. You say true, 'tis so
   indeed. If such tricks as these strip you out of your
   lieutenantry, it had been better you had not kissed your
   three fingers so oft, which now again you are most apt   170
   to play the sir in. Very good: well kissed, an excellent
   courtesy! 'Tis so indeed. Yet again your fingers to your
   lips? Would they were clyster-pipes for your sake!
      Trumpet
   (*Aloud*) The Moor! I know his trumpet.
CASSIO   'Tis truly so.
DESDEMONA
   Let's meet him and receive him.
CASSIO   Lo, where he comes!
      Enter Othello and attendants
OTHELLO
   O, my fair warrior!
DESDEMONA   My dear Othello!
OTHELLO
   It gives me wonder great as my content
   To see you here before me. O, my soul's joy!
   If after every tempest come such calms,
   May the winds blow till they have wakened death,   180

And let the labouring bark climb hills of seas,
Olympus-high, and duck again as low
As hell's from heaven. If it were now to die,
'Twere now to be most happy; for I fear
My soul hath her content so absolute
That not another comfort like to this
Succeeds in unknown fate.

DESDEMONA   The heavens forbid
But that our loves and comforts should increase,
Even as our days do grow.

OTHELLO   Amen to that, sweet Powers!
190   I cannot speak enough of this content;
It stops me here; it is too much of joy.
    They kiss
And this, and this the greatest discords be
That e'er our hearts shall make.

IAGO (*aside*)   O, you are well tuned now!
But I'll set down the pegs that make this music,
As honest as I am.

OTHELLO   Come, let's to the castle.
News, friends; our wars are done; the Turks are drowned.
How does my old acquaintance of this isle?
Honey, you shall be well desired in Cyprus:
I have found great love amongst them. O my sweet,
200   I prattle out of fashion and I dote
In mine own comforts. I prithee, good Iago,
Go to the bay and disembark my coffers;
Bring thou the Master to the citadel;
He is a good one, and his worthiness
Does challenge much respect. Come, Desdemona,
Once more well met at Cyprus!
                    Exeunt all except Iago and Roderigo
IAGO (*to soldiers, who go off*) Do thou meet me presently at
the harbour. (*To Roderigo*) Come hither. If thou be'st

valiant – as they say base men being in love have then a
nobility in their natures more than is native to them –   210
list me. The Lieutenant tonight watches on the court of
guard. First, I must tell thee this: Desdemona is directly
in love with him.

RODERIGO With him? Why, 'tis not possible!

IAGO Lay thy finger thus, and let thy soul be instructed.
Mark me with what violence she first loved the Moor,
but for bragging and telling her fantastical lies. And
will she love him still for prating? Let not thy discreet
heart think it. Her eye must be fed. And what delight
shall she have to look on the devil? When the blood is   220
made dull with the act of sport, there should be, again
to inflame it and give satiety a fresh appetite, loveliness
in favour, sympathy in years, manners and beauties: all
which the Moor is defective in. Now for want of these
required conveniences, her delicate tenderness will find
itself abused, begin to heave the gorge, disrelish and
abhor the Moor. Very nature will instruct her in it and
compel her to some second choice. Now, sir, this granted
– as it is a most pregnant and unforced position – who
stands so eminently in the degree of this fortune as   230
Cassio does? – a knave very voluble; no further conscionable than in putting on the mere form of civil and
humane seeming for the better compassing of his salt
and most hidden loose affection. Why, none; why, none
– a slipper and subtle knave, a finder out of occasions;
that has an eye can stamp and counterfeit advantages,
though true advantage never present itself; a devilish
knave! Besides, the knave is handsome, young, and hath
all those requisites in him that folly and green minds
look after. A pestilent complete knave; and the woman   240
hath found him already.

RODERIGO I cannot believe that in her: she's full of most
blessed condition.

IAGO Blessed fig's end! The wine she drinks is made of
grapes. If she had been blessed, she would never have
loved the Moor. Blessed pudding! Didst thou not see her
paddle with the palm of his hand? Didst not mark that?

RODERIGO Yes, that I did: but that was but courtesy.

IAGO Lechery, by this hand: an index and obscure prologue to the history of lust and foul thoughts. They met
so near with their lips that their breaths embraced
together. Villainous thoughts, Roderigo! When these
mutualities so marshal the way, hard at hand comes the
master and main exercise, th'incorporate conclusion.
Pish! But, sir, be you ruled by me. I have brought you
from Venice. Watch you tonight: for the command, I'll
lay't upon you. Cassio knows you not; I'll not be far
from you. Do you find some occasion to anger Cassio,
either by speaking too loud, or tainting his discipline, or
from what other course you please, which the time shall
more favourably minister.

RODERIGO Well.

IAGO Sir, he's rash and very sudden in choler, and haply
with his truncheon may strike at you: provoke him that
he may, for even out of that will I cause these of Cyprus
to mutiny, whose qualification shall come into no true
taste again but by the displanting of Cassio. So shall you
have a shorter journey to your desires by the means I
shall then have to prefer them, and the impediment most
profitably removed, without the which there were no
expectation of our prosperity.

RODERIGO I will do this, if you can bring it to any opportunity.

IAGO I warrant thee. Meet me by and by at the citadel. I
must fetch his necessaries ashore. Farewell.

RODERIGO Adieu.   *Exit*

IAGO

    That Cassio loves her, I do well believe't:
    That she loves him, 'tis apt and of great credit.
    The Moor – howbeit that I endure him not –
    Is of a constant, loving, noble nature,   280
    And, I dare think, he'll prove to Desdemona
    A most dear husband. Now, I do love her too;
    Not out of absolute lust – though peradventure
    I stand accountant for as great a sin –
    But partly led to diet my revenge
    For that I do suspect the lusty Moor
    Hath leaped into my seat, the thought whereof
    Doth, like a poisonous mineral, gnaw my inwards,
    And nothing can, or shall, content my soul
    Till I am evened with him, wife for wife;   290
    Or failing so, yet that I put the Moor
    At least into a jealousy so strong
    That judgement cannot cure. Which thing to do
    If this poor trash of Venice, whom I leash
    For his quick hunting, stand the putting on,
    I'll have our Michael Cassio on the hip,
    Abuse him to the Moor in the rank garb –
    For I fear Cassio with my night-cap too –
    Make the Moor thank me, love me, and reward me
    For making him egregiously an ass,   300
    And practising upon his peace and quiet,
    Even to madness. 'Tis here, but yet confused:
    Knavery's plain face is never seen till used.   *Exit*

    Enter Herald, with a proclamation   **II.2**

HERALD It is Othello's pleasure, our noble and valiant
    General, that upon certain tidings now arrived importing

the mere perdition of the Turkish fleet, every man put himself into triumph: some to dance, some to make bonfires, each man to what sport and revels his addiction leads him. For, besides these beneficial news, it is the celebration of his nuptial. So much was his pleasure should be proclaimed. All offices are open, and there is full liberty of feasting from this present hour of five till the bell have told eleven. Heaven bless the isle of Cyprus and our noble General Othello!   *Exit*

II.3   *Enter Othello, Desdemona, Cassio, and attendants*

OTHELLO
Good Michael, look you to the guard tonight.
Let's teach ourselves that honourable stop,
Not to outsport discretion.

CASSIO
Iago hath direction what to do;
But, notwithstanding, with my personal eye
Will I look to't.

OTHELLO   Iago is most honest.
Michael, good night. Tomorrow with your earliest
Let me have speech with you. (*To Desdemona*)
        Come, my dear love,
The purchase made, the fruits are to ensue:
That profit's yet to come 'tween me and you.
Good night.
                Exeunt Othello, Desdemona, and attendants
        Enter Iago
CASSIO Welcome, Iago; we must to the watch.
IAGO Not this hour, Lieutenant; 'tis not yet ten o'th'clock. Our General cast us thus early for the love of his Desdemona; who let us not therefore blame. He hath

not yet made wanton the night with her; and she is
sport for Jove.

CASSIO She is a most exquisite lady.

IAGO And, I'll warrant her, full of game.

CASSIO Indeed, she is a most fresh and delicate creature.   20

IAGO What an eye she has! Methinks it sounds a parley to
provocation.

CASSIO An inviting eye, and yet methinks right modest.

IAGO And when she speaks, is it not an alarum to love?

CASSIO She is indeed perfection.

IAGO Well, happiness to their sheets! Come, Lieutenant,
I have a stoup of wine; and here without are a brace of
Cyprus gallants that would fain have a measure to the
health of black Othello.

CASSIO Not tonight, good Iago. I have very poor and   30
unhappy brains for drinking. I could well wish courtesy
would invent some other custom of entertainment.

IAGO O, they are our friends! But one cup; I'll drink for
you.

CASSIO I have drunk but one cup tonight, and that was
craftily qualified too; and behold what innovation it
makes here. I am unfortunate in the infirmity and dare
not task my weakness with any more.

IAGO What, man! 'Tis a night of revels; the gallants desire
it.   40

CASSIO Where are they?

IAGO Here, at the door: I pray you call them in.

CASSIO I'll do't, but it dislikes me.   *Exit*

IAGO
    If I can fasten but one cup upon him,
    With that which he hath drunk tonight already,
    He'll be as full of quarrel and offence
    As my young mistress' dog. Now my sick fool Roderigo,
    Whom love hath turned almost the wrong side out,

To Desdemona hath tonight caroused
50 Potations pottle-deep; and he's to watch.
Three else of Cyprus, noble swelling spirits —
That hold their honours in a wary distance,
The very elements of this warlike isle —
Have I tonight flustered with flowing cups,
And they watch too. Now 'mongst this flock of drunkards,
Am I to put our Cassio in some action
That may offend the isle. But here they come;
If consequence do but approve my dream,
My boat sails freely both with wind and stream.

>   *Enter Cassio with Montano and Gentlemen, and*
>   *servants with wine*

60 CASSIO 'Fore God, they have given me a rouse already.
MONTANO Good faith, a little one; not past a pint, as I am
a soldier.
IAGO Some wine, ho!
(*Sings*)   And let me the canakin clink, clink;
               And let me the canakin clink;
                   A soldier's a man
                   O, man's life's but a span;
               Why, then, let a soldier drink.
Some wine, boys.
70 CASSIO 'Fore God, an excellent song.
IAGO I learned it in England, where indeed they are most
potent in potting. Your Dane, your German, and your
swag-bellied Hollander — drink, ho! — are nothing to
your English.
CASSIO Is your Englishman so expert in his drinking?
IAGO Why, he drinks you with facility your Dane dead
drunk; he sweats not to overthrow your Almaine; he
gives your Hollander a vomit, ere the next pottle can be
filled.
80 CASSIO To the health of our General!

MONTANO I am for it, Lieutenant; and I'll do you justice.

IAGO O, sweet England!
   (*Sings*) King Stephen was and-a worthy peer,
            His breeches cost him but a crown;
          He held them sixpence all too dear;
            With that he called the tailor lown.
          He was a wight of high renown,
            And thou art but of low degree;
          'Tis pride that pulls the country down;   90
            Then take thine auld cloak about thee.
   Some wine, ho!

CASSIO 'Fore God, this is a more exquisite song than the
other.

IAGO Will you hear't again?

CASSIO No, for I hold him to be unworthy of his place
that does those things. Well, God's above all; and there
be souls must be saved, and there be souls must not be
saved.

IAGO It's true, good Lieutenant.   100

CASSIO For mine own part – no offence to the General,
nor any man of quality – I hope to be saved.

IAGO And so do I too, Lieutenant.

CASSIO Ay, but, by your leave, not before me. The
Lieutenant is to be saved before the Ancient. Let's have
no more of this; let's to our affairs. God forgive us our
sins. Gentlemen, let's look to our business. Do not
think, gentlemen, I am drunk: this is my Ancient, this
is my right hand, and this is my left. I am not drunk
now: I can stand well enough and I speak well enough.   110

GENTLEMEN Excellent well.

CASSIO Why, very well; you must not think then that I
am drunk.   *Exit*

MONTANO To th'platform, masters; come, let's set the
    watch.
IAGO
    You see this fellow that is gone before:
    He is a soldier, fit to stand by Caesar
    And give direction; and do but see his vice:
    'Tis to his virtue a just equinox,
120   The one as long as th'other. 'Tis pity of him.
    I fear the trust Othello puts in him,
    On some odd time of his infirmity,
    Will shake this island.
MONTANO   But is he often thus?
IAGO
    'Tis evermore the prologue to his sleep:
    He'll watch the horologe a double set,
    If drink rock not his cradle.
MONTANO   It were well
    The General were put in mind of it:
    Perhaps he sees it not, or his good nature
    Prizes the virtue that appears in Cassio
130   And looks not on his evils. Is not this true?
        Enter Roderigo
IAGO
    (*aside*) How now, Roderigo!
    I pray you after the Lieutenant go!   *Exit Roderigo*
MONTANO
    And 'tis great pity that the noble Moor
    Should hazard such a place as his own second
    With one of an ingraft infirmity.
    It were an honest action to say
    So to the Moor.
IAGO   Not I, for this fair island!
    I do love Cassio well and would do much
    To cure him of this evil.

(Cry within) 'Help! Help!'

> But hark, what noise?

Enter Cassio, pursuing Roderigo

CASSIO Zounds, you rogue, you rascal!   140

MONTANO What's the matter, Lieutenant?

CASSIO A knave teach me my duty? I'll beat the knave into
a twiggen-bottle.

RODERIGO Beat me?

CASSIO Dost thou prate, rogue?

He strikes Roderigo

MONTANO Nay, good Lieutenant; I pray you, sir, hold
your hand.

CASSIO Let me go, sir, or I'll knock you o'er the mazzard.

MONTANO Come, come, you're drunk.

CASSIO Drunk!   150

IAGO *(to Roderigo)* Away, I say; go out and cry a mutiny.

> *Exit Roderigo*

Nay, good Lieutenant. God's will, gentleman!
Help, ho! Lieutenant! Sir! Montano! Sir!
Help, masters. Here's a goodly watch indeed.

Bell rings

Who's that which rings the bell? Diablo, ho!
The town will rise. God's will, Lieutenant, hold!
You will be shamed for ever!

Enter Othello and attendants

OTHELLO

What is the matter here?

MONTANO   Zounds, I bleed still.

I am hurt to th'death.

OTHELLO   Hold for your lives!

IAGO

Hold, ho, Lieutenant, sir, Montano, gentlemen!   160
Have you forgot all sense of place and duty?
Hold! The General speaks to you: hold, for shame!

OTHELLO
    Why, how now, ho! From whence ariseth this?
    Are we turned Turks and to ourselves do that
    Which heaven hath forbid the Ottomites?
    For Christian shame, put by this barbarous brawl.
    He that stirs next to carve for his own rage
    Holds his soul light: he dies upon his motion.
    Silence that dreadful bell: it frights the isle
170   From her propriety. What is the matter, masters?
    Honest Iago, that looks dead with grieving,
    Speak, who began this? On thy love I charge thee.

IAGO
    I do not know. Friends all but now, even now,
    In quarter and in terms like bride and groom
    Devesting them for bed: and then but now –
    As if some planet had unwitted men –
    Swords out, and tilting one at others' breasts
    In opposition bloody. I cannot speak
    Any beginning to this peevish odds;
180   And would in action glorious I had lost
    Those legs that brought me to a part of it.

OTHELLO
    How comes it, Michael, you are thus forgot?

CASSIO
    I pray you pardon me: I cannot speak.

OTHELLO
    Worthy Montano, you were wont to be civil:
    The gravity and stillness of your youth
    The world hath noted; and your name is great
    In mouths of wisest censure. What's the matter
    That you unlace your reputation thus
    And spend your rich opinion for the name
190   Of a night-brawler? Give me answer to it.

MONTANO

    Worthy Othello, I am hurt to danger.
    Your officer, Iago, can inform you,
    While I spare speech, which something now offends me,
    Of all that I do know; nor know I aught
    By me that's said or done amiss this night,
    Unless self-charity be sometimes a vice,
    And to defend ourselves it be a sin
    When violence assails us.

OTHELLO   Now, by heaven,

    My blood begins my safer guides to rule,
    And passion, having my best judgement collied,   200
    Assays to lead the way. Zounds, if I stir,
    Or do but lift this arm, the best of you
    Shall sink in my rebuke. Give me to know
    How this foul rout began, who set it on;
    And he that is approved in this offence,
    Though he had twinned with me, both at a birth,
    Shall lose me. What! In a town of war
    Yet wild, the people's hearts brimful of fear,
    To manage private and domestic quarrel
    In night, and on the court and guard of safety,   210
    'Tis monstrous. Iago, who began't?

MONTANO

    If partially affined or leagued in office,
    Thou dost deliver more or less than truth,
    Thou art no soldier.

IAGO   Touch me not so near.

    I had rather have this tongue cut from my mouth
    Than it should do offence to Michael Cassio.
    Yet, I persuade myself, to speak the truth
    Shall nothing wrong him. This it is, General.
    Montano and myself being in speech,
    There comes a fellow, crying out for help,   220

And Cassio following with determined sword
To execute upon him. Sir, this gentleman
Steps in to Cassio and entreats his pause:
Myself the crying fellow did pursue
Lest by his clamour – as it so fell out –
The town might fall in fright. He, swift of foot,
Outran my purpose and I returned the rather
For that I heard the clink and fall of swords
And Cassio high in oath, which till tonight
230 I ne'er might say before. When I came back –
For this was brief – I found them close together
At blow and thrust, even as again they were
When you yourself did part them.
More of this matter can I not report:
But men are men; the best sometimes forget.
Though Cassio did some little wrong to him,
As men in rage strike those that wish them best,
Yet surely Cassio, I believe, received
From him that fled some strange indignity
240 Which patience could not pass.
OTHELLO   I know, Iago,
Thy honesty and love doth mince this matter,
Making it light to Cassio. Cassio, I love thee,
But nevermore be officer of mine.
  Enter Desdemona, attended
Look, if my gentle love be not raised up.
I'll make thee an example.
DESDEMONA   What is the matter, dear?
OTHELLO
All's well now, sweeting: come away to bed.
Sir, for your hurts myself will be your surgeon.
        Montano is led off
Iago, look with care about the town
And silence those whom this vile brawl distracted.

Come, Desdemona, 'tis the soldiers' life   250
To have their balmy slumbers waked with strife.
                    Exeunt all but Iago and Cassio
IAGO What, are you hurt, Lieutenant?
CASSIO Ay, past all surgery.
IAGO Marry, God forbid!
CASSIO Reputation, reputation, reputation! O, I have lost
    my reputation! I have lost the immortal part of myself,
    and what remains is bestial. My reputation, Iago, my
    reputation!
IAGO As I am an honest man I thought you had received
    some bodily wound: there is more of sense in that   260
    than in reputation. Reputation is an idle and most false
    imposition; oft got without merit and lost without
    deserving. You have lost no reputation at all, unless you
    repute yourself such a loser. What, man! There are
    ways to recover the General again. You are but now cast
    in his mood — a punishment more in policy than in
    malice — even so as one would beat his offenceless dog to
    affright an imperious lion. Sue to him again, and he's
    yours.
CASSIO I will rather sue to be despised than to deceive so   270
    good a commander with so slight, so drunken, and so
    indiscreet an officer. Drunk! And speak parrot! And
    squabble! Swagger! Swear! And discourse fustian with
    one's own shadow! O, thou invisible spirit of wine, if
    thou hast no name to be known by, let us call thee devil.
IAGO What was he that you followed with your sword?
    What had he done to you?
CASSIO I know not.
IAGO Is't possible?
CASSIO I remember a mass of things, but nothing dis-   280
    tinctly: a quarrel, but nothing wherefore. O God, that
    men should put an enemy in their mouths to steal away

their brains! That we should with joy, pleasance, revel
and applause transform ourselves into beasts!

IAGO Why, but you are now well enough! How came you
thus recovered?

CASSIO It hath pleased the devil drunkenness to give place
to the devil wrath: one unperfectness shows me another,
to make me frankly despise myself.

290 IAGO Come, you are too severe a moraller. As the time,
the place and the condition of this country stands, I
could heartily wish this had not so befallen: but since
it is as it is, mend it for your own good.

CASSIO I will ask him for my place again; he shall tell me
I am a drunkard. Had I as many mouths as Hydra, such
an answer would stop them all. To be now a sensible
man, by and by a fool, and presently a beast! O, strange!
Every inordinate cup is unblessed and the ingredience
is a devil.

300 IAGO Come, come; good wine is a good familiar creature if
it be well used: exclaim no more against it. And, good
Lieutenant, I think you think I love you.

CASSIO I have well approved it, sir. I drunk!

IAGO You or any man living may be drunk at a time, man.
I'll tell you what you shall do. Our General's wife is
now the General. I may say so in this respect, for that
he hath devoted and given up himself to the contempla-
tion, mark, and denotement of her parts and graces.
Confess yourself freely to her; importune her help to
310 put you in your place again. She is of so free, so kind, so
apt, so blessed a disposition, that she holds it a vice in her
goodness not to do more than she is requested. This
broken joint between you and her husband, entreat her
to splinter; and my fortunes against any lay worth
naming, this crack of your love shall grow stronger than
it was before.

CASSIO You advise me well.

IAGO I protest in the sincerity of love and honest kindness.

CASSIO I think it freely; and betimes in the morning I will   320
beseech the virtuous Desdemona to undertake for me.
I am desperate of my fortunes if they check me here.

IAGO You are in the right. Good night, Lieutenant, I must
to the watch.

CASSIO Good night, honest Iago.   *Exit*

IAGO
And what's he then that says I play the villain,
When this advice is free I give, and honest,
Probal to thinking, and indeed the course
To win the Moor again? For 'tis most easy
Th'inclining Desdemona to subdue   330
In any honest suit. She's framed as fruitful
As the free elements; and then for her
To win the Moor, were't to renounce his baptism,
All seals and symbols of redeemèd sin,
His soul is so enfettered to her love,
That she may make, unmake, do what she list,
Even as her appetite shall play the god
With his weak function. How am I then a villain
To counsel Cassio to this parallel course
Directly to his good? Divinity of hell!   340
When devils will the blackest sins put on,
They do suggest at first with heavenly shows
As I do now. For whiles this honest fool
Plies Desdemona to repair his fortunes
And she for him pleads strongly to the Moor,
I'll pour this pestilence into his ear:
That she repeals him for her body's lust,
And by how much she strives to do him good,
She shall undo her credit with the Moor.

350 So will I turn her virtue into pitch,
And out of her own goodness make the net
That shall enmesh them all.
   Enter Roderigo
                          How now, Roderigo?
RODERIGO I do follow here in the chase, not like a hound
that hunts, but one that fills up the cry. My money is
almost spent; I have been tonight exceedingly well
cudgelled; and I think the issue will be, I shall have so
much experience for my pains; and so, with no money
at all, and a little more wit, return again to Venice.
IAGO
How poor are they that have not patience!
360 What wound did ever heal but by degrees?
Thou know'st we work by wit, and not by witchcraft,
And wit depends on dilatory time.
Does't not go well? Cassio hath beaten thee,
And thou by that small hurt hath cashiered Cassio.
Though other things grow fair against the sun,
Yet fruits that blossom first will first be ripe.
Content thyself awhile. By th'mass, 'tis morning:
Pleasure and action make the hours seem short.
Retire thee; go where thou art billeted.
370 Away, I say, thou shalt know more hereafter:
Nay, get thee gone.   *Exit Roderigo*
                 Two things are to be done.
My wife must move for Cassio to her mistress:
I'll set her on.
Myself the while to draw the Moor apart,
And bring him jump when he may Cassio find
Soliciting his wife. Ay, that's the way.
Dull not device by coldness and delay.   *Exit*

*

Enter Cassio and Musicians   III.I

CASSIO

Masters, play here – I will content your pains –
Something that's brief; and bid 'Good morrow, General'.
They play
Enter Clown

CLOWN Why, masters, have your instruments been in
Naples, that they speak i'th'nose thus?

FIRST MUSICIAN How, sir, how?

CLOWN Are these, I pray you, wind instruments?

FIRST MUSICIAN Ay, marry are they, sir.

CLOWN O, thereby hangs a tail.

FIRST MUSICIAN Whereby hangs a tale, sir?

CLOWN Marry, sir, by many a wind instrument that I   10
know. But, masters, here's money for you: and the
General so likes your music that he desires you, for
love's sake, to make no more noise with it.

FIRST MUSICIAN Well, sir, we will not.

CLOWN If you have any music that may not be heard,
to't again. But, as they say, to hear music the General
does not greatly care.

FIRST MUSICIAN We have none such, sir.

CLOWN Then put up your pipes in your bag, for I'll
away. Go, vanish into air, away.   *Exeunt Musicians*   20

CASSIO Dost thou hear, mine honest friend?

CLOWN No, I hear not your honest friend: I hear you.

CASSIO Prithee keep up thy quillets – there's a poor piece
of gold for thee. If the gentlewoman that attends the
General's wife be stirring, tell her there's one Cassio
entreats her a little favour of speech. Wilt thou do this?

CLOWN She is stirring, sir. If she will stir hither, I shall
seem to notify unto her.

CASSIO Do, good my friend.   *Exit Clown*

Enter Iago

30   In happy time, Iago.

IAGO   You have not been abed then?

CASSIO
Why, no: the day had broke before we parted.
I have made bold, Iago,
To send in to your wife. My suit to her
Is that she will to virtuous Desdemona
Procure me some access.

IAGO   I'll send her to you presently;
And I'll devise a mean to draw the Moor
Out of the way, that your converse and business
May be more free.

CASSIO   I humbly thank you for't.

                                                    Exit Iago

I never knew a Florentine more kind and honest.
Enter Emilia

EMILIA
40   Good morrow, good Lieutenant; I am sorry
For your displeasure: but all will sure be well.
The General and his wife are talking of it,
And she speaks for you stoutly. The Moor replies
That he you hurt is of great fame in Cyprus,
And great affinity; and that in wholesome wisdom
He might not but refuse you; but he protests he loves you
And needs no other suitor but his likings
To take the safest occasion by the front
To bring you in again.

CASSIO   Yet I beseech you,
50   If you think fit, or that it may be done,
Give me advantage of some brief discourse
With Desdemona alone.

EMILIA   Pray you, come in:

I will bestow you where you shall have time
To speak your bosom freely.

CASSIO   I am much bound to you.

Exeunt

Enter Othello, Iago, and Gentlemen   III.2

OTHELLO
These letters give, Iago, to the pilot,
And by him do my duties to the senate.
That done, I will be walking on the works:
Repair there to me.

IAGO   Well, my good lord, I'll do't. *Exit*

OTHELLO
This fortification, gentlemen, shall we see't?

GENTLEMEN
We'll wait upon your lordship.   *Exeunt*

Enter Desdemona, Cassio, and Emilia   III.3

DESDEMONA
Be thou assured, good Cassio, I will do
All my abilities in thy behalf.

EMILIA
Good madam, do: I warrant it grieves my husband
As if the case were his.

DESDEMONA
O, that's an honest fellow! Do not doubt, Cassio,
But I will have my lord and you again
As friendly as you were.

CASSIO   Bounteous madam,
Whatever shall become of Michael Cassio,
He's never anything but your true servant.

DESDEMONA

10   I know't: I thank you. You do love my lord;
    You have known him long, and be you well assured
    He shall in strangeness stand no farther off
    Than in a politic distance.

CASSIO   Ay, but, lady,

    That policy may either last so long,
    Or feed upon such nice and waterish diet,
    Or breed itself so out of circumstance,
    That I being absent and my place supplied,
    My General will forget my love and service.

DESDEMONA

    Do not doubt that. Before Emilia here,
20   I give thee warrant of thy place. Assure thee,
    If I do vow a friendship, I'll perform it
    To the last article. My lord shall never rest.
    I'll watch him tame and talk him out of patience;
    His bed shall seem a school, his board a shrift;
    I'll intermingle everything he does
    With Cassio's suit. Therefore be merry, Cassio,
    For thy solicitor shall rather die
    Than give thy cause away.

        Enter Othello and Iago

EMILIA

    Madam, here comes my lord.

CASSIO

30   Madam, I'll take my leave.

DESDEMONA

    Why, stay and hear me speak.

CASSIO

    Madam, not now: I am very ill at ease,
    Unfit for mine own purposes.

DESDEMONA

    Well, do your discretion.   *Exit Cassio*

IAGO

Ha! I like not that.

OTHELLO   What dost thou say?

IAGO

Nothing, my lord; or if — I know not what.

OTHELLO

Was not that Cassio parted from my wife?

IAGO

Cassio, my lord? No, sure, I cannot think it

That he would sneak away so guilty-like,

Seeing you coming.

OTHELLO   I do believe 'twas he.   40

DESDEMONA

How now, my lord?

I have been talking with a suitor here,

A man that languishes in your displeasure.

OTHELLO

Who is't you mean?

DESDEMONA

Why, your Lieutenant, Cassio. Good my lord,

If I have any grace or power to move you,

His present reconciliation take.

For if he be not one that truly loves you,

That errs in ignorance, and not in cunning,

I have no judgement in an honest face.   50

I prithee call him back.

OTHELLO   Went he hence now?

DESDEMONA

Yes, faith; so humbled

That he hath left part of his grief with me

To suffer with him. Good love, call him back.

OTHELLO

Not now, sweet Desdemon; some other time.

DESDEMONA
    But shall't be shortly?
OTHELLO   The sooner, sweet, for you.
DESDEMONA
    Shall't be tonight, at supper?
OTHELLO   No, not tonight.
DESDEMONA
    Tomorrow dinner then?
OTHELLO   I shall not dine at home.
    I meet the captains at the citadel.
DESDEMONA
60 Why, then, tomorrow night, or Tuesday morn,
    On Tuesday noon, or night; on Wednesday morn.
    I prithee name the time, but let it not
    Exceed three days. In faith, he's penitent:
    And yet his trespass in our common reason –
    Save that, they say, the wars must make example
    Out of their best – is not almost a fault
    T'incur a private check. When shall he come?
    Tell me, Othello. I wonder in my soul
    What you would ask me that I should deny,
70 Or stand so mammering on? What! Michael Cassio,
    That came a-wooing with you? And so many a time –
    When I have spoke of you dispraisingly –
    Hath ta'en your part, to have so much to do
    To bring him in? By'r Lady, I could do much.
OTHELLO
    Prithee, no more: let him come when he will;
    I will deny thee nothing.
DESDEMONA   Why, this is not a boon:
    'Tis as I should entreat you wear your gloves
    Or feed on nourishing dishes, or keep you warm,
    Or sue to you to do a peculiar profit
80 To your own person. Nay, when I have a suit

Wherein I mean to touch your love indeed
It shall be full of poise and difficult weight,
And fearful to be granted.

OTHELLO   I will deny thee nothing.
Whereon, I do beseech thee, grant me this:
To leave me but a little to my self.

DESDEMONA
Shall I deny you? No; farewell, my lord.

OTHELLO
Farewell, my Desdemona, I'll come to thee straight.

DESDEMONA
Emilia, come. Be as your fancies teach you.
Whate'er you be, I am obedient.

                              Exeunt Desdemona and Emilia

OTHELLO
Excellent wretch! Perdition catch my soul   90
But I do love thee! And when I love thee not,
Chaos is come again.

IAGO   My noble lord —

OTHELLO
What dost thou say, Iago?

IAGO   Did Michael Cassio,
When you wooed my lady, know of your love?

OTHELLO
He did, from first to last. Why dost thou ask?

IAGO
But for a satisfaction of my thought —
No further harm.

OTHELLO   Why of thy thought, Iago?

IAGO
I did not think he had been acquainted with her.

OTHELLO
O yes, and went between us very oft.

IAGO

100   Indeed!

OTHELLO

Indeed? Ay, indeed. Discern'st thou aught in that?
Is he not honest?

IAGO   Honest, my lord?

OTHELLO   Honest? Ay, honest.

IAGO

My lord, for aught I know.

OTHELLO   What dost thou think?

IAGO

Think, my lord?

OTHELLO

Think, my lord! By heaven, he echoes me,
As if there were some monster in his thought
Too hideous to be shown. Thou dost mean something.
I heard thee say even now, thou lik'st not that,
When Cassio left my wife. What didst not like?

110   And when I told thee he was of my counsel
In my whole course of wooing, thou cried'st 'Indeed!'
And didst contract and purse thy brow together,
As if thou then hadst shut up in thy brain
Some horrible conceit. If thou dost love me,
Show me thy thought.

IAGO

My lord, you know I love you.

OTHELLO   I think thou dost:
And for I know thou'rt full of love and honesty,
And weigh'st thy words before thou giv'st them breath,
Therefore these stops of thine affright me more:

120   For such things in a false disloyal knave
Are tricks of custom; but in a man that's just,
They're close dilations, working from the heart,
That passion cannot rule.

IAGO   For Michael Cassio,
  I dare be sworn I think that he is honest.
OTHELLO
  I think so too.
IAGO   Men should be what they seem;
  Or those that be not, would they might seem none!
OTHELLO
  Certain, men should be what they seem.
IAGO
  Why, then, I think Cassio's an honest man.
OTHELLO
  Nay, yet there's more in this.
  I prithee speak to me as to thy thinkings,   130
  As thou dost ruminate, and give thy worst of thoughts
  The worst of words.
IAGO   Good my lord, pardon me;
  Though I am bound to every act of duty,
  I am not bound to that all slaves are free to:
  Utter my thoughts. Why, say they are vile and false?
  As where's that palace whereinto foul things
  Sometimes intrude not? Who has a breast so pure,
  But some uncleanly apprehensions
  Keep leets and law-days, and in session sit
  With meditations lawful?   140
OTHELLO
  Thou dost conspire against thy friend, Iago,
  If thou but think'st him wronged, and mak'st his ear
  A stranger to thy thoughts.
IAGO   I do beseech you,
  Though I perchance am vicious in my guess –
  As I confess it is my nature's plague
  To spy into abuses, and of my jealousy
  Shapes faults that are not – that your wisdom then,
  From one that so imperfectly conjects,

Would take no notice, nor build yourself a trouble
150   Out of his scattering and unsure observance.
It were not for your quiet nor your good,
Nor for my manhood, honesty, and wisdom,
To let you know my thoughts.
OTHELLO   What dost thou mean?
IAGO
Good name in man and woman, dear my lord,
Is the immediate jewel of their souls.
Who steals my purse, steals trash; 'tis something, nothing;
'Twas mine, 'tis his, and has been slave to thousands:
But he that filches from me my good name
Robs me of that which not enriches him
160   And makes me poor indeed.
OTHELLO   By heaven, I'll know thy thoughts.
IAGO
You cannot, if my heart were in your hand,
Nor shall not, whilst 'tis in my custody.
OTHELLO
Ha!
IAGO   O, beware, my lord, of jealousy!
It is the green-eyed monster, which doth mock
The meat it feeds on. That cuckold lives in bliss
Who certain of his fate loves not his wronger,
But O, what damnèd minutes tells he o'er,
Who dotes yet doubts, suspects yet fondly loves!
OTHELLO
O misery!
IAGO
170   Poor and content is rich, and rich enough;
But riches fineless is as poor as winter,
To him that ever fears he shall be poor.
Good God, the souls of all my tribe defend
From jealousy!

OTHELLO   Why, why is this?
    Think'st thou I'd make a life of jealousy,
    To follow still the changes of the moon
    With fresh suspicions? No, to be once in doubt
    Is once to be resolved. Exchange me for a goat,
    When I shall turn the business of my soul
    To such exsufflicate and blown surmises,   180
    Matching thy inference. 'Tis not to make me jealous
    To say my wife is fair, loves company,
    Is free of speech, sings, plays, and dances well:
    Where virtue is, these are more virtuous.
    Nor from mine own weak merits will I draw
    The smallest fear or doubt of her revolt,
    For she had eyes and chose me. No, Iago,
    I'll see before I doubt; when I doubt, prove;
    And on the proof, there is no more but this:
    Away at once with love or jealousy!   190

IAGO
    I am glad of this: for now I shall have reason
    To show the love and duty that I bear you
    With franker spirit. Therefore, as I am bound,
    Receive it from me. I speak not yet of proof.
    Look to your wife; observe her well with Cassio.
    Wear your eye thus: not jealous, nor secure.
    I would not have your free and noble nature,
    Out of self-bounty, be abused. Look to't.
    I know our country disposition well:
    In Venice they do let God see the pranks   200
    They dare not show their husbands; their best conscience
    Is not to leave't undone, but keep't unknown.

OTHELLO
    Dost thou say so?

IAGO
    She did deceive her father, marrying you,

And when she seemed to shake, and fear your looks,
She loved them most.

OTHELLO   And so she did.

IAGO   Why, go to, then!
She that so young could give out such a seeming,
To seel her father's eyes up close as oak –
He thought 'twas witchcraft. – But I am much to blame,
210   I humbly do beseech you of your pardon
For too much loving you.

OTHELLO   I am bound to thee for ever.

IAGO
I see this hath a little dashed your spirits.

OTHELLO
Not a jot, not a jot.

IAGO   In faith, I fear it has.
I hope you will consider what is spoke
Comes from my love. But I do see you're moved.
I am to pray you, not to strain my speech
To grosser issues, nor to larger reach
Than to suspicion.

OTHELLO
I will not.

IAGO   Should you do so, my lord,
220   My speech should fall into such vile success
Which my thoughts aimed not at. Cassio's my worthy
          friend.
My lord, I see you're moved.

OTHELLO   No, not much moved.
I do not think but Desdemona's honest.

IAGO
Long live she so! And long live you to think so!

OTHELLO
And yet, how nature erring from itself –

IAGO
   Ay, there's the point: as, to be bold with you,
   Not to affect many proposèd matches
   Of her own clime, complexion, and degree,
   Whereto we see in all things nature tends,
   Foh! One may smell in such a will most rank,   230
   Foul disproportion, thoughts unnatural.
   But, pardon me, I do not in position
   Distinctly speak of her, though I may fear
   Her will, recoiling to her better judgement,
   May fall to match you with her country forms,
   And happily repent.
OTHELLO   Farewell, farewell.
   If more thou dost perceive, let me know more.
   Set on thy wife to observe. Leave me, Iago.
IAGO
   (*going*) My lord, I take my leave.
OTHELLO
   Why did I marry? This honest creature doubtless   240
   Sees and knows more, much more than he unfolds.
IAGO
   (*returning*) My lord, I would I might entreat your honour
   To scan this thing no farther. Leave it to time.
   Although 'tis fit that Cassio have his place,
   For sure he fills it up with great ability,
   Yet, if you please to hold him off awhile,
   You shall by that perceive him and his means;
   Note if your lady strain his entertainment
   With any strong or vehement importunity –
   Much will be seen in that. In the meantime,   250
   Let me be thought too busy in my fears,
   As worthy cause I have to fear I am,
   And hold her free, I do beseech your honour.

OTHELLO
　　Fear not my government.
IAGO　　　　　　　　　I once more take my leave. *Exit*
OTHELLO
　　This fellow's of exceeding honesty,
　　And knows all qualities with a learnèd spirit
　　Of human dealings. If I do prove her haggard,
　　Though that her jesses were my dear heart-strings,
　　I'd whistle her off, and let her down the wind
260　　To prey at fortune. Haply, for I am black
　　And have not those soft parts of conversation
　　That chamberers have; or for I am declined
　　Into the vale of years – yet that's not much –
　　She's gone: I am abused, and my relief
　　Must be to loathe her. O, curse of marriage!
　　That we can call these delicate creatures ours
　　And not their appetites! I had rather be a toad
　　And live upon the vapour of a dungeon
　　Than keep a corner in the thing I love
270　　For others' uses. Yet 'tis the plague of great ones;
　　Prerogatived are they less than the base.
　　'Tis destiny unshunnable, like death:
　　Even then this forkèd plague is fated to us
　　When we do quicken. Desdemona comes:
　　　　Enter Desdemona and Emilia
　　If she be false, O, then heaven mocks itself!
　　I'll not believe't.
DESDEMONA　　　　How now, my dear Othello!
　　Your dinner, and the generous islanders
　　By you invited, do attend your presence.
OTHELLO
　　I am to blame.
DESDEMONA　　　Why do you speak so faintly?
280　　Are you not well?

OTHELLO
　　I have a pain upon my forehead here.

DESDEMONA
　　Faith, that's with watching: 'twill away again.
　　Let me but bind it hard, within this hour
　　It will be well.

OTHELLO　　　　Your napkin is too little.
　　　He puts the handkerchief from him, and she drops it
　　Let it alone. Come, I'll go in with you.

DESDEMONA
　　I am very sorry that you are not well.
　　　　　　　　　　Exeunt Othello and Desdemona

EMILIA
　　I am glad I have found this napkin:
　　This was her first remembrance from the Moor.
　　My wayward husband hath a hundred times
　　Wooed me to steal it; but she so loves the token –　　290
　　For he conjured her she should ever keep it –
　　That she reserves it evermore about her
　　To kiss and talk to. I'll have the work ta'en out,
　　And give 't Iago.
　　What he will do with it, heaven knows, not I:
　　I nothing, but to please his fantasy.
　　　Enter Iago

IAGO
　　How now? What do you here alone?

EMILIA
　　Do not you chide: I have a thing for you.

IAGO
　　A thing for me? It is a common thing.

EMILIA
　　Ha!　　　　　　　　　　　　　　　　　　　　　300

IAGO
　　To have a foolish wife.

EMILIA

O, is that all? What will you give me now
For that same handkerchief?

IAGO   What handkerchief?

EMILIA

What handkerchief!
Why that the Moor first gave to Desdemona;
That which so often you did bid me steal.

IAGO

Hast stol'n it from her?

EMILIA

No, faith, she let it drop by negligence,
And to th'advantage, I, being here, took't up.
Look, here it is.

IAGO   A good wench! Give it me.

EMILIA

What will you do with't, that you have been so earnest
To have me filch it?

IAGO (*snatching it*)   Why, what is that to you?

EMILIA

If it be not for some purpose of import,
Give't me again. Poor lady, she'll run mad
When she shall lack it.

IAGO

Be not acknown on't: I have use for it.
Go, leave me.   *Exit Emilia*
I will in Cassio's lodging lose this napkin,
And let him find it. Trifles light as air
Are to the jealous confirmations strong
As proofs of holy writ. This may do something.
The Moor already changes with my poison.
Dangerous conceits are in their natures poisons,
Which at the first are scarce found to distaste,

But, with a little act upon the blood,
Burn like the mines of sulphur.
   Enter Othello
                              I did say so.
Look where he comes! Not poppy, nor mandragora,
Nor all the drowsy syrups of the world,
Shall ever medicine thee to that sweet sleep
Which thou owed'st yesterday.

OTHELLO   Ha, ha, false to me!   330

IAGO

Why, how now, General! No more of that.

OTHELLO

Avaunt! Be gone! Thou hast set me on the rack.
I swear 'tis better to be much abused,
Than but to know't a little.

IAGO   How now, my lord!

OTHELLO

What sense had I of her stolen hours of lust?
I saw't not, thought it not, it harmed not me.
I slept the next night well, was free and merry;
I found not Cassio's kisses on her lips.
He that is robbed, not wanting what is stolen,
Let him not know't, and he's not robbed at all.   340

IAGO

I am sorry to hear this.

OTHELLO

I had been happy if the general camp,
Pioners and all, had tasted her sweet body,
So I had nothing known. O, now, for ever
Farewell the tranquil mind! Farewell content!
Farewell the plumèd troops and the big wars
That make ambition virtue – O, farewell!
Farewell the neighing steed, and the shrill trump,
The spirit-stirring drum, th'ear-piercing fife,

350   The royal banner and all quality,
       Pride, pomp and circumstance of glorious war!
       And, O you mortal engines, whose rude throats
       Th'immortal Jove's dread clamours counterfeit,
       Farewell! Othello's occupation's gone.

IAGO
       Is't possible, my lord?

OTHELLO
       Villain, be sure thou prove my love a whore;
       Be sure of it: give me the ocular proof,
       Or by the worth of mine eternal soul,
       Thou hadst been better have been born a dog
360   Than answer my waked wrath!

IAGO   Is't come to this?

OTHELLO
       Make me to see't: or, at the least, so prove it
       That the probation bear no hinge nor loop
       To hang a doubt on – or woe upon thy life!

IAGO
       My noble lord –

OTHELLO
       If thou dost slander her and torture me,
       Never pray more; abandon all remorse;
       On horror's head horrors accumulate;
       Do deeds to make heaven weep, all earth amazed:
       For nothing canst thou to damnation add
370   Greater than that.

IAGO   O grace! O heaven defend me!
       Are you a man? Have you a soul? Or sense?
       God bu'y you: take mine office. O wretched fool,
       That lov'st to make thine honesty a vice!
       O monstrous world! Take note, take note, O world!
       To be direct and honest is not safe.
       I thank you for this profit, and from hence

I'll love no friend, sith love breeds such offence.

OTHELLO

Nay, stay: thou shouldst be honest.

IAGO

I should be wise; for honesty's a fool
And loses that it works for.

OTHELLO   By the world,   380
I think my wife be honest, and think she is not;
I think that thou art just, and think thou art not.
I'll have some proof. Her name that was as fresh
As Dian's visage is now begrimed and black
As mine own face. If there be cords or knives,
Poison or fire or suffocating streams,
I'll not endure it. Would I were satisfied!

IAGO

I see, sir, you are eaten up with passion.
I do repent me that I put it to you.
You would be satisfied?

OTHELLO   Would! Nay, I will.   390

IAGO

And may. But how? How satisfied, my lord?
Would you, the supervisor, grossly gape on?
Behold her topped?

OTHELLO   Death and damnation! O!

IAGO

It were a tedious difficulty, I think,
To bring them to that prospect. Damn them then
If ever mortal eyes do see them bolster
More than their own! What then? How then?
What shall I say? Where's satisfaction?
It is impossible you should see this,
Were they as prime as goats, as hot as monkeys,   400
As salt as wolves in pride, and fools as gross
As ignorance made drunk. But yet, I say,

If imputation and strong circumstance,
Which lead directly to the door of truth,
Will give you satisfaction, you might have't.

OTHELLO
Give me a living reason she's disloyal.

IAGO
I do not like the office.
But sith I am entered in this cause so far –
Pricked to't by foolish honesty and love –
410   I will go on. I lay with Cassio lately,
And being troubled with a raging tooth
I could not sleep.
There are a kind of men so loose of soul
That in their sleeps will mutter their affairs:
One of this kind is Cassio.
In sleep I heard him say: 'Sweet Desdemona,
Let us be wary, let us hide our loves';
And then, sir, would he gripe and wring my hand,
Cry 'O sweet creature!' and then kiss me hard,
420   As if he plucked up kisses by the roots,
That grew upon my lips; then laid his leg
Over my thigh, and sighed and kissed, and then
Cried 'Cursèd fate that gave thee to the Moor!'

OTHELLO
O monstrous! Monstrous!

IAGO   Nay, this was but his dream.

OTHELLO
But this denoted a foregone conclusion.

IAGO
'Tis a shrewd doubt, though it be but a dream:
And this may help to thicken other proofs
That do demonstrate thinly.

OTHELLO   I'll tear her all to pieces!

IAGO

    Nay, but be wise: yet we see nothing done,

    She may be honest yet. Tell me but this: 430

    Have you not sometimes seen a handkerchief,

    Spotted with strawberries, in your wife's hand?

OTHELLO

    I gave her such a one: 'twas my first gift.

IAGO

    I know not that: but such a handkerchief —

    I am sure it was your wife's — did I today

    See Cassio wipe his beard with.

OTHELLO   If it be that —

IAGO

    If it be that, or any that was hers,

    It speaks against her with the other proofs.

OTHELLO

    O, that the slave had forty thousand lives!

    One is too poor, too weak for my revenge.   440

    Now do I see 'tis true. Look here, Iago —

    All my fond love thus do I blow to heaven:

    'Tis gone.

    Arise, black vengeance, from thy hollow cell!

    Yield up, O love, thy crown and hearted throne

    To tyrannous hate! Swell, bosom, with thy fraught,

    For 'tis of aspics' tongues!

IAGO   Yet be content.

OTHELLO

    O, blood, blood, blood!

IAGO

    Patience, I say: your mind perhaps may change.

OTHELLO

    Never, Iago. Like to the Pontic sea,   450

    Whose icy current and compulsive course

    Ne'er feels retiring ebb, but keeps due on

To the Propontic and the Hellespont,
Even so my bloody thoughts with violent pace
Shall ne'er look back, ne'er ebb to humble love,
Till that a capable and wide revenge
Swallow them up. Now, by yond marble heaven,
In the due reverence of a sacred vow
I here engage my words.
> *He kneels*

IAGO   Do not rise yet.
> *He kneels*

460   Witness you ever-burning lights above,
You elements, that clip us round about,
Witness that here Iago doth give up
The execution of his wit, hands, heart,
To wronged Othello's service. Let him command,
And to obey shall be in me remorse,
What bloody business ever.
> *They rise*

OTHELLO   I greet thy love,
Not with vain thanks, but with acceptance bounteous;
And will upon the instant put thee to't.
Within these three days let me hear thee say
470   That Cassio's not alive.

IAGO   My friend is dead;
'Tis done at your request. But let her live.

OTHELLO
Damn her, lewd minx! O, damn her, damn her!
Come go with me apart. I will withdraw
To furnish me with some swift means of death
For the fair devil. Now art thou my Lieutenant.

IAGO
I am your own for ever.   *Exeunt*

Enter Desdemona, Emilia, and Clown   III.4

DESDEMONA Do you know, sirrah, where Lieutenant
   Cassio lies?

CLOWN I dare not say he lies anywhere.

DESDEMONA Why, man?

CLOWN He's a soldier, and for one to say a soldier lies is
   stabbing.

DESDEMONA Go to! Where lodges he?

CLOWN To tell you where he lodges is to tell you where I
   lie.

DESDEMONA Can anything be made of this?   10

CLOWN I know not where he lodges, and for me to devise a
   lodging, and say he lies here, or he lies there, were to lie
   in mine own throat.

DESDEMONA Can you inquire him out? And be edified by
   report?

CLOWN I will catechize the world for him, that is, make
   questions, and by them answer.

DESDEMONA Seek him; bid him come hither; tell him I
   have moved my lord on his behalf, and hope all will be
   well.   20

CLOWN To do this is within the compass of man's wit, and
   therefore I will attempt the doing of it.   *Exit*

DESDEMONA
Where should I lose that handkerchief, Emilia?

EMILIA
I know not, madam.

DESDEMONA
Believe me, I had rather have lost my purse
Full of crusadoes; and, but my noble Moor
Is true of mind, and made of no such baseness
As jealous creatures are, it were enough
To put him to ill-thinking.

EMILIA   Is he not jealous?

DESDEMONA

30   Who? He? I think the sun where he was born
        Drew all such humours from him.

EMILIA   Look where he comes.

Enter Othello

DESDEMONA

        I will not leave him now till Cassio
        Be called to him. How is't with you, my lord?

OTHELLO

        Well, my good lady. (*Aside*) O, hardness to dissemble!
        How do you, Desdemona?

DESDEMONA   Well, my good lord.

OTHELLO

        Give me your hand. This hand is moist, my lady.

DESDEMONA

        It yet has felt no age, nor known no sorrow.

OTHELLO

        This argues fruitfulness and liberal heart.
        Hot, hot and moist. This hand of yours requires

40   A sequester from liberty, fasting and prayer,
        Much castigation, exercise devout;
        For there's a young and sweating devil here
        That commonly rebels. 'Tis a good hand,
        A frank one.

DESDEMONA   You may, indeed, say so:
        For 'twas that hand that gave away my heart.

OTHELLO

        A liberal hand! The hearts of old gave hands;
        But our new heraldry is hands, not hearts.

DESDEMONA

        I cannot speak of this. Come now, your promise.

OTHELLO

        What promise, chuck?

DESDEMONA
   I have sent to bid Cassio come speak with you.   50
OTHELLO
   I have a salt and sorry rheum offends me:
   Lend me thy handkerchief.
DESDEMONA   Here, my lord.
OTHELLO
   That which I gave you.
DESDEMONA   I have it not about me.
OTHELLO
   Not?
DESDEMONA No, faith, my lord.
OTHELLO   That is a fault.
   That handkerchief
   Did an Egyptian to my mother give:
   She was a charmer and could almost read
   The thoughts of people. She told her, while she kept it,
   'Twould make her amiable and subdue my father
   Entirely to her love; but, if she lost it   60
   Or made a gift of it, my father's eye
   Should hold her loathèd, and his spirits should hunt
   After new fancies. She, dying, gave it me,
   And bid me, when my fate would have me wive,
   To give it her. I did so; and take heed on't:
   Make it a darling, like your precious eye.
   To lose or give't away were such perdition
   As nothing else could match.
DESDEMONA   Is't possible?
OTHELLO
   'Tis true: there's magic in the web of it.
   A sibyl, that had numbered in the world   70
   The sun to course two hundred compasses,
   In her prophetic fury sewed the work:
   The worms were hallowed that did breed the silk,

And it was dyed in mummy, which the skilful
Conserved of maidens' hearts.

DESDEMONA   Indeed! Is't true?

OTHELLO
Most veritable; therefore look to't well.

DESDEMONA
Then would to God that I had never seen it!

OTHELLO
Ha! Wherefore?

DESDEMONA
Why do you speak so startingly and rash?

OTHELLO
80   Is't lost? Is't gone? Speak: is't out o'th'way?

DESDEMONA
Heaven bless us!

OTHELLO   Say you?

DESDEMONA   It is not lost.
But what an if it were?

OTHELLO   How!

DESDEMONA
I say it is not lost.

OTHELLO   Fetch't: let me see't.

DESDEMONA
Why, so I can, sir; but I will not now.
This is a trick to put me from my suit.
Pray you let Cassio be received again.

OTHELLO
Fetch me the handkerchief: my mind misgives.

DESDEMONA
Come, come:
You'll never meet a more sufficient man.

OTHELLO
90   The handkerchief!

DESDEMONA   I pray, talk me of Cassio.

OTHELLO

The handkerchief!

DESDEMONA   A man that all his time

Hath founded his good fortunes on your love;

Shared dangers with you –

OTHELLO

The handkerchief!

DESDEMONA   I'faith you are to blame.

OTHELLO

Zounds!   *Exit*

EMILIA

Is not this man jealous?

DESDEMONA   I ne'er saw this before.

Sure, there's some wonder in this handkerchief:

I am most unhappy in the loss of it.

EMILIA

'Tis not a year or two shows us a man.

They are all but stomachs, and we all but food;   100

They eat us hungerly, and when they are full,

They belch us. Look you, Cassio and my husband.

Enter Iago and Cassio

IAGO

There is no other way: 'tis she must do't.

And lo, the happiness! Go, and importune her.

DESDEMONA

How now, good Cassio! What's the news with you?

CASSIO

Madam, my former suit. I do beseech you

That by your virtuous means I may again

Exist and be a member of his love,

Whom I, with all the office of my heart,

Entirely honour. I would not be delayed.   110

If my offence be of such mortal kind

That nor my service past, nor present sorrow,

Nor purposed merit in futurity,
Can ransom me into his love again,
But to know so must be my benefit:
So shall I clothe me in a forced content,
And shut myself up in some other course
To Fortune's alms.

DESDEMONA   Alas, thrice-gentle Cassio!
My advocation is not now in tune:
My lord is not my lord; nor should I know him,
Were he in favour as in humour altered.
So help me every spirit sanctified
As I have spoken for you all my best,
And stood within the blank of his displeasure
For my free speech! You must awhile be patient.
What I can do, I will; and more I will,
Than for myself I dare. Let that suffice you.

IAGO
Is my lord angry?

EMILIA   He went hence but now
And certainly in strange unquietness.

IAGO
Can he be angry? I have seen the cannon
When it hath blown his ranks into the air,
And like the devil from his very arm
Puffed his own brother — and can he be angry?
Something of moment then. I will go meet him.
There's matter in't indeed if he be angry.

DESDEMONA
I prithee do so.   *Exit Iago*
            Something, sure, of state,
Either from Venice, or some unhatched practice
Made demonstrable here in Cyprus to him,
Hath puddled his clear spirit; and in such cases
Men's natures wrangle with inferior things,

Though great ones are their object. 'Tis even so.
For let our finger ache, and it endues
Our healthful members even to that sense
Of pain. Nay, we must think men are not gods,
Nor of them look for such observancy
As fits the bridal. Beshrew me much, Emilia,
I was – unhandsome warrior as I am –
Arraigning his unkindness with my soul;
But now I find I had suborned the witness
And he's indicted falsely.   150

EMILIA

Pray heaven it be state matters, as you think,
And no conception nor no jealous toy
Concerning you.

DESDEMONA

Alas the day, I never gave him cause.

EMILIA

But jealous souls will not be answered so;
They are not ever jealous for the cause,
But jealous for they're jealous. It is a monster
Begot upon itself, born on itself.

DESDEMONA

Heaven keep that monster from Othello's mind.

EMILIA

Lady, amen!   160

DESDEMONA

I will go seek him. Cassio, walk here about.
If I do find him fit, I'll move your suit,
And seek to effect it to my uttermost.

CASSIO

I humbly thank your ladyship.

Exeunt Desdemona and Emilia

Enter Bianca

BIANCA

    'Save you, friend Cassio.

CASSIO   What make you from home?

    How is it with you, my most fair Bianca?

    I'faith, sweet love, I was coming to your house.

BIANCA

    And I was going to your lodging, Cassio.

    What! Keep a week away? Seven days and nights?

170   Eight score eight hours? And lovers' absent hours

    More tedious than the dial eight score times!

    O weary reckoning!

CASSIO   Pardon me, Bianca.

    I have this while with leaden thoughts been pressed:

    But I shall in a more continuate time

    Strike off this score of absence. Sweet Bianca,

    Take me this work out.

BIANCA   O Cassio, whence came this?

    This is some token from a newer friend.

    To the felt absence now I feel a cause.

    Is't come to this? Well, well.

CASSIO   Go to, woman!

180   Throw your vile guesses in the devil's teeth

    From whence you have them. You are jealous now

    That this is from some mistress, some remembrance:

    No, by my faith, Bianca.

BIANCA   Why, whose is it?

CASSIO

    I know not, sweet. I found it in my chamber.

    I like the work well. Ere it be demanded –

    As like enough it will – I'd have it copied.

    Take it and do't, and leave me for this time.

BIANCA

    Leave you? Wherefore?

CASSIO
   I do attend here on the General,
   And think it no addition, nor my wish,   190
   To have him see me womaned.
BIANCA   Why, I pray you?
CASSIO
   Not that I love you not.
BIANCA   But that you do not love me.
   I pray you, bring me on the way a little,
   And say if I shall see you soon at night.
CASSIO
   'Tis but a little way that I can bring you,
   For I attend here: but I'll see you soon.
BIANCA
   'Tis very good: I must be circumstanced.   *Exeunt*

*

   Enter Othello and Iago   IV.I
IAGO
   Will you think so?
OTHELLO   Think so, Iago?
IAGO   What!
   To kiss in private?
OTHELLO   An unauthorized kiss.
IAGO
   Or to be naked with her friend in bed
   An hour or more, not meaning any harm?
OTHELLO
   Naked in bed, Iago, and not mean harm?
   It is hypocrisy against the devil.
   They that mean virtuously and yet do so,
   The devil their virtue tempts, and they tempt heaven.

IAGO

So they do nothing, 'tis a venial slip.

10 But if I give my wife a handkerchief —

OTHELLO

What then?

IAGO

Why, then, 'tis hers, my lord, and being hers,

She may, I think, bestow't on any man.

OTHELLO

She is protectress of her honour too.

May she give that?

IAGO

Her honour is an essence that's not seen:

They have it very oft that have it not.

But for the handkerchief —

OTHELLO

By heaven, I would most gladly have forgot it!

20 Thou said'st — O, it comes o'er my memory

As doth the raven o'er the infected house,

Boding to all! — he had my handkerchief.

IAGO

Ay, what of that?

OTHELLO   That's not so good now.

IAGO   What

If I had said, I had seen him do you wrong,

Or heard him say — as knaves be such abroad,

Who having by their own importunate suit

Or voluntary dotage of some mistress

Convincèd or supplied them, cannot choose

But they must blab —

OTHELLO   Hath he said anything?

IAGO

30 He hath, my lord; but be you well assured,

No more than he'll unswear.

OTHELLO   What hath he said?
IAGO
Faith, that he did – I know not what he did.
OTHELLO
What? What?
IAGO
Lie –
OTHELLO With her?
IAGO   With her, on her, what you will.
OTHELLO Lie with her? Lie on her? We say lie on her
when they belie her. Lie with her! Zounds, that's ful-
some! Handkerchief – confession – handkerchief! To
confess and be hanged for his labour. First to be hanged
and then to confess! I tremble at it. Nature would not
invest herself in such shadowing passion without some   40
instruction. It is not words that shakes me thus! Pish!
Noses, ears, and lips! Is't possible? – Confess? Handker-
chief! O devil!
      He falls
IAGO
Work on,
My medicine, work! Thus credulous fools are caught,
And many worthy and chaste dames even thus,
All guiltless, meet reproach. What ho, my lord!
My lord, I say! Othello!
      Enter Cassio
                              How now, Cassio!
CASSIO
What's the matter?
IAGO
My lord is fallen into an epilepsy.   50
This is his second fit: he had one yesterday.
CASSIO
Rub him about the temples.

IAGO   No, forbear.
The lethargy must have his quiet course.
If not, he foams at mouth; and by and by
Breaks out to savage madness. Look, he stirs.
Do you withdraw yourself a little while:
He will recover straight. When he is gone,
I would on great occasion speak with you.

Exit Cassio

How is it, General? Have you not hurt your head?

OTHELLO

60 Dost thou mock me?

IAGO   I mock you? No, by heaven!
Would you would bear your fortune like a man!

OTHELLO

A hornèd man's a monster and a beast.

IAGO

There's many a beast then in a populous city,
And many a civil monster.

OTHELLO

Did he confess it?

IAGO   Good sir, be a man.
Think every bearded fellow that's but yoked
May draw with you. There's millions now alive
That nightly lie in those unproper beds
Which they dare swear peculiar. Your case is better.

70 O, 'tis the spite of hell, the fiend's arch-mock,
To lip a wanton in a secure couch,
And to suppose her chaste! No, let me know;
And knowing what I am, I know what shall be.

OTHELLO

O, thou art wise, 'tis certain.

IAGO   Stand you awhile apart;
Confine yourself but in a patient list.
Whilst you were here, o'erwhelmèd with your grief —

A passion most unsuiting such a man –
Cassio came hither. I shifted him away
And laid good scuse upon your ecstasy;
Bade him anon return and here speak with me,   80
The which he promised. Do but encave yourself,
And mark the fleers, the gibes, and notable scorns
That dwell in every region of his face.
For I will make him tell the tale anew,
Where, how, how oft, how long ago, and when
He hath, and is again, to cope your wife.
I say, but mark his gestures. Marry, patience!
Or I shall say you're all in all in spleen
And nothing of a man.

OTHELLO   Dost thou hear, Iago?
I will be found most cunning in my patience,   90
But – dost thou hear? – most bloody.

IAGO   That's not amiss,
But yet keep time in all. Will you withdraw?

                                        Othello retires

Now will I question Cassio of Bianca,
A housewife, that by selling her desires
Buys herself bread and clothes. It is a creature
That dotes on Cassio – as 'tis the strumpet's plague
To beguile many and be beguiled by one.
He, when he hears of her, cannot refrain
From the excess of laughter. Here he comes.

    Enter Cassio

As he shall smile, Othello shall go mad;   100
And his unbookish jealousy must construe
Poor Cassio's smiles, gestures, and light behaviour
Quite in the wrong. How do you now, Lieutenant?

CASSIO
The worser that you give me the addition
Whose want even kills me.

IAGO

    Ply Desdemona well and you are sure on't.

    Now if this suit lay in Bianca's power,

    How quickly should you speed!

CASSIO   Alas, poor caitiff!

OTHELLO

    (*aside*) Look, how he laughs already!

IAGO

110   I never knew a woman love man so.

CASSIO

    Alas, poor rogue! I think i'faith she loves me.

OTHELLO

    (*aside*) Now he denies it faintly, and laughs it out.

IAGO

    Do you hear, Cassio?

OTHELLO

    (*aside*) Now he importunes him to tell it o'er.

    Go to, well said, well said!

IAGO

    She gives it out that you shall marry her.

    Do you intend it?

CASSIO

    Ha, ha, ha!

OTHELLO

    (*aside*) Do you triumph, Roman? Do you triumph?

120 CASSIO I marry her! What! A customer! Prithee bear some
    charity to my wit: do not think it so unwholesome. Ha,
    ha, ha!

OTHELLO (*aside*) So, so, so, so: they laugh that win.

IAGO Faith, the cry goes that you shall marry her.

CASSIO Prithee, say true.

IAGO I am a very villain else.

OTHELLO (*aside*) Have you scored me? Well.

CASSIO This is the monkey's own giving out. She is

persuaded I will marry her out of her own love and
flattery, not out of my promise.   130
OTHELLO (*aside*) Iago beckons me. Now he begins the
story.
CASSIO She was here even now. She haunts me in every
place. I was the other day talking on the sea-bank with
certain Venetians, and thither comes the bauble and, by
this hand, falls me thus about my neck.
OTHELLO (*aside*) Crying 'O dear Cassio!' as it were. His
gesture imports it.
CASSIO So hangs and lolls and weeps upon me, so hales
and pulls me. Ha, ha, ha!   140
OTHELLO (*aside*) Now he tells how she plucked him to
my chamber. O, I see that nose of yours, but not that
dog I shall throw it to!
CASSIO Well, I must leave her company.
IAGO Before me! Look where she comes.
CASSIO 'Tis such another fitchew! Marry, a perfumed one!
     Enter Bianca
What do you mean by this haunting of me?
BIANCA Let the devil and his dam haunt you! What did
you mean by that same handkerchief you gave me even
now? I was a fine fool to take it. I must take out the   150
work! A likely piece of work, that you should find it in
your chamber, and not know who left it there! This is
some minx's token, and I must take out the work?
There, give it your hobby-horse, wheresover you had
it. I'll take out no work on't.
CASSIO How now, my sweet Bianca! How now, how now!
OTHELLO (*aside*) By heaven, that should be my handkerchief!
BIANCA If you'll come to supper tonight, you may. If you
will not, come when you are next prepared for. *Exit*   160
IAGO After her, after her!

CASSIO Faith I must: she'll rail in the street else.

IAGO Will you sup there?

CASSIO Faith, I intend to.

IAGO Well, I may chance to see you: for I would very fain speak with you.

CASSIO Prithee come, will you?

IAGO Go to! Say no more.   *Exit Cassio*

OTHELLO (*coming forward*) How shall I murder him, Iago?

170   IAGO Did you perceive how he laughed at his vice?

OTHELLO O, Iago!

IAGO And did you see the handkerchief?

OTHELLO Was that mine?

IAGO Yours, by this hand! And to see how he prizes the foolish woman your wife: she gave it him, and he hath giv'n it his whore.

OTHELLO I would have him nine years a-killing! – A fine woman, a fair woman, a sweet woman!

IAGO Nay, you must forget that.

180   OTHELLO Ay, let her rot and perish, and be damned tonight, for she shall not live! No, my heart is turned to stone: I strike it, and it hurts my hand. – O, the world hath not a sweeter creature! She might lie by an emperor's side and command him tasks.

IAGO Nay, that's not your way.

OTHELLO Hang her! I do but say what she is: so delicate with her needle, an admirable musician! O, she will sing the savageness out of a bear! Of so high and plenteous wit and invention!

190   IAGO She's the worse for all this.

OTHELLO O, a thousand, thousand times! – And then of so gentle a condition.

IAGO Ay, too gentle.

OTHELLO Nay, that's certain – but yet the pity of it, Iago! O, Iago, the pity of it, Iago!

IAGO If you are so fond over her iniquity, give her patent
to offend, for if it touch not you, it comes near nobody.

OTHELLO I will chop her into messes! Cuckold me!

IAGO O, 'tis foul in her!   200

OTHELLO With mine officer!

IAGO That's fouler.

OTHELLO Get me some poison, Iago, this night. I'll not
expostulate with her, lest her body and beauty unprovide
my mind again – this night, Iago.

IAGO Do it not with poison; strangle her in her bed, even
the bed she hath contaminated.

OTHELLO Good, good! The justice of it pleases; very
good!

IAGO And for Cassio, let me be his undertaker. You shall   210
hear more by midnight.

OTHELLO
Excellent good!
    Trumpet sounds
                        What trumpet is that same?

IAGO
I warrant, something from Venice.
    Enter Lodovico, Desdemona, and attendants
                        'Tis Lodovico,
Come from the Duke; and see your wife is with him.

LODOVICO
God save you, worthy General!

OTHELLO   With all my heart, sir.

LODOVICO
The Duke and Senators of Venice greet you.
    He gives him a letter

OTHELLO
I kiss the instrument of their pleasures.
    He reads the letter

DESDEMONA

And what's the news, good cousin Lodovico?

IAGO

I am very glad to see you, signor:
220   Welcome to Cyprus.

LODOVICO

I thank you. How does Lieutenant Cassio?

IAGO

Lives, sir.

DESDEMONA

Cousin, there's fallen between him and my lord
An unkind breach; but you shall make all well.

OTHELLO

Are you sure of that?

DESDEMONA

My lord?

OTHELLO

'This fail you not to do, as you will' –

LODOVICO

He did not call: he's busy in the paper.
Is there division 'twixt my lord and Cassio?

DESDEMONA

230   A most unhappy one; I would do much
T'atone them, for the love I bear to Cassio.

OTHELLO

Fire and brimstone!

DESDEMONA

My lord?

OTHELLO

Are you wise?

DESDEMONA

What, is he angry?

LODOVICO   Maybe the letter moved him.
For, as I think, they do command him home,

Deputing Cassio in his government.

DESDEMONA

  By my troth, I am glad on't.

OTHELLO   Indeed!

DESDEMONA   My lord?

OTHELLO

  I am glad to see you mad.

DESDEMONA   Why, sweet Othello!

OTHELLO

  Devil!   240

  He strikes her

DESDEMONA

  I have not deserved this.

LODOVICO

  My lord, this would not be believed in Venice,
  Though I should swear I saw't. 'Tis very much.
  Make her amends; she weeps.

OTHELLO   O devil, devil!

  If that the earth could teem with woman's tears,
  Each drop she falls would prove a crocodile.
  Out of my sight!

DESDEMONA   I will not stay to offend you.

LODOVICO

  Truly an obedient lady.
  I do beseech your lordship call her back.

OTHELLO

  Mistress!   250

DESDEMONA

  My lord?

OTHELLO

  What would you with her, sir?

LODOVICO

  Who? I, my lord?

OTHELLO

Ay, you did wish that I would make her turn.
Sir, she can turn, and turn, and yet go on,
And turn again. And she can weep, sir, weep.
And she's obedient; as you say, obedient,
Very obedient – proceed you in your tears –
Concerning this, sir – O, well-painted passion! –
260   I am commanded home – get you away!
I'll send for you anon. – Sir, I obey the mandate,
And will return to Venice. – Hence, avaunt!

Exit Desdemona

Cassio shall have my place. And sir, tonight
I do entreat that we may sup together.
You are welcome, sir, to Cyprus. Goats and monkeys!

Exit

LODOVICO

Is this the noble Moor, whom our full senate
Call all-in-all sufficient? Is this the nature
Whom passion could not shake? Whose solid virtue
The shot of accident nor dart of chance
270   Could neither graze nor pierce?

IAGO   He is much changed.

LODOVICO

Are his wits safe? Is he not light of brain?

IAGO

He's that he is: I may not breathe my censure
What he might be. If what he might he is not,
I would to heaven he were.

LODOVICO   What! Strike his wife!

IAGO

Faith, that was not so well: yet would I knew
That stroke would prove the worst!

LODOVICO   Is it his use?
Or did the letters work upon his blood

And new-create this fault?

IAGO   Alas, alas!
It is not honesty in me to speak
What I have seen and known. You shall observe him,   280
And his own courses will denote him so,
That I may save my speech. Do but go after,
And mark how he continues.

LODOVICO
I am sorry that I am deceived in him.   *Exeunt*

Enter Othello and Emilia   IV.2

OTHELLO
You have seen nothing then?

EMILIA
Nor ever heard, nor ever did suspect.

OTHELLO
Yes, you have seen Cassio and she together.

EMILIA
But then I saw no harm; and then I heard
Each syllable that breath made up between them.

OTHELLO
What! Did they never whisper?

EMILIA   Never, my lord.

OTHELLO
Nor send you out o'th'way?

EMILIA   Never.

OTHELLO
To fetch her fan, her gloves, her mask, nor nothing?

EMILIA
Never, my lord.

OTHELLO
That's strange.   10

EMILIA

    I durst, my lord, to wager she is honest,
    Lay down my soul at stake. If you think other,
    Remove your thought: it doth abuse your bosom.
    If any wretch have put this in your head,
    Let heaven requite it with the serpent's curse!
    For if she be not honest, chaste, and true,
    There's no man happy. The purest of their wives
    Is foul as slander.

OTHELLO   Bid her come hither: go!

                              Exit Emilia

    She says enough; yet she's a simple bawd
20   That cannot say as much. This is a subtle whore,
    A closet lock and key of villainous secrets;
    And yet she'll kneel and pray – I have seen her do't.

    Enter Desdemona and Emilia

DESDEMONA

    My lord, what is your will?

OTHELLO   Pray, chuck, come hither.

DESDEMONA

    What is your pleasure?

OTHELLO   Let me see your eyes.
    Look in my face.

DESDEMONA   What horrible fancy's this?

OTHELLO (*to Emilia*)

    Some of your function, mistress.
    Leave procreants alone and shut the door.
    Cough or cry 'hem' if anybody come.
    Your mystery, your mystery! Nay, dispatch! *Exit Emilia*

DESDEMONA

30   Upon my knees, what doth your speech import?
    I understand a fury in your words,
    But not the words.

OTHELLO   Why, what art thou?

DESDEMONA

Your wife, my lord; your true and loyal wife.

OTHELLO

Come, swear it; damn thyself;
Lest being like one of heaven, the devils themselves
Should fear to seize thee. Therefore be double-damned:
Swear thou art honest.

DESDEMONA   Heaven doth truly know it.

OTHELLO

Heaven truly knows that thou art false as hell.

DESDEMONA

To whom, my lord? With whom? How am I false?

OTHELLO

Ah, Desdemon! Away, away, away!   40

DESDEMONA

Alas, the heavy day! Why do you weep?
Am I the motive of these tears my lord?
If haply you my father do suspect
An instrument of this your calling back,
Lay not your blame on me. If you have lost him,
I have lost him too.

OTHELLO   Had it pleased heaven
To try me with affliction, had they rained
All kind of sores and shames on my bare head,
Steeped me in poverty to the very lips,
Given to captivity me and my utmost hopes,   50
I should have found in some place of my soul
A drop of patience. But alas, to make me
A fixèd figure for the time of scorn
To point his slow unmoving finger at!
Yet could I bear that too, well, very well:
But there where I have garnered up my heart,
Where either I must live, or bear no life,
The fountain from the which my current runs,

Or else dries up – to be discarded thence
60   Or keep it as a cistern for foul toads
To knot and gender in! Turn thy complexion there,
Patience, thou young and rose-lipped cherubin,
Ay, there look grim as hell!

DESDEMONA
I hope my noble lord esteems me honest.

OTHELLO
O, ay! As summer flies are in the shambles,
That quicken even with blowing, O, thou weed,
Who art so lovely fair, and smell'st so sweet
That the sense aches at thee, would thou hadst ne'er
    been born!

DESDEMONA
Alas, what ignorant sin have I committed?

OTHELLO
70   Was this fair paper, this most goodly book,
Made to write 'whore' upon? What committed!
Committed? O, thou public commoner!
I should make very forges of my cheeks,
That would to cinders burn up modesty,
Did I but speak thy deeds. What committed?
Heaven stops the nose at it, and the moon winks;
The bawdy wind, that kisses all it meets,
Is hushed within the hollow mine of earth
And will not hear it. What committed?
80   Impudent strumpet!

DESDEMONA   By heaven, you do me wrong.

OTHELLO
Are you not a strumpet?

DESDEMONA   No, as I am a Christian.
If to preserve this vessel for my lord
From any other foul unlawful touch,
Be not to be a strumpet, I am none.

OTHELLO
    What! Not a whore?
DESDEMONA   No, as I shall be saved.
OTHELLO
    Is't possible?
DESDEMONA
    O, heaven forgive us!
OTHELLO   I cry you mercy then:
    I took you for that cunning whore of Venice
    That married with Othello. (*Calling*) You, mistress,
    That have the office opposite to Saint Peter   90
    And keep the gate of hell!
        Enter Emilia
                                You, you, ay, you!
    We have done our course: there's money for your pains.
    I pray you turn the key, and keep our counsel.   *Exit*
EMILIA
    Alas, what does this gentleman conceive?
    How do you, madam? How do you, my good lady?
DESDEMONA
    Faith, half asleep.
EMILIA
    Good madam, what's the matter with my lord?
DESDEMONA
    With who?
EMILIA
    Why, with my lord, madam.
DESDEMONA
    Who is thy lord?
EMILIA   He that is yours, sweet lady.   100
DESDEMONA
    I have none. Do not talk to me, Emilia:
    I cannot weep; nor answers have I none,
    But what should go by water. Prithee tonight

Lay on my bed my wedding sheets, remember,
And call thy husband hither.

EMILIA   Here's a change indeed!

Exit

DESDEMONA

'Tis meet I should be used so, very meet.
How have I been behaved, that he might stick
The smallest opinion on my least misuse?

Enter Emilia and Iago

IAGO

What is your pleasure, madam? How is't with you?

DESDEMONA

110   I cannot tell: those that do teach young babes
Do it with gentle means and easy tasks:
He might have chid me so, for, in good faith,
I am a child to chiding.

IAGO   What is the matter, lady?

EMILIA

Alas, Iago, my lord hath so bewhored her,
Thrown such despite and heavy terms upon her
As true heart cannot bear.

DESDEMONA

Am I that name, Iago?

IAGO   What name, fair lady?

DESDEMONA

Such as she said my lord did say I was.

EMILIA

He called her whore: a beggar in his drink

120   Could not have laid such terms upon his callet.

IAGO

Why did he so?

DESDEMONA

I do not know: I am sure I am none such.

IAGO

Do not weep, do not weep. Alas the day!

EMILIA

Hath she forsook so many noble matches,
Her father, and her country, all her friends,
To be called whore? Would it not make one weep?

DESDEMONA

It is my wretched fortune.

IAGO   Beshrew him for't!
How comes this trick upon him?

DESDEMONA   Nay, heaven doth know.

EMILIA

I will be hanged if some eternal villain,
Some busy and insinuating rogue,   130
Some cogging, cozening slave, to get some office,
Have not devised this slander; I'll be hanged else.

IAGO

Fie, there is no such man! It is impossible.

DESDEMONA

If any such there be, heaven pardon him.

EMILIA

A halter pardon him and hell gnaw his bones!
Why should he call her whore? Who keeps her company?
What place, what time, what form, what likelihood?
The Moor's abused by some most villainous knave,
Some base notorious knave, some scurvy fellow.
O heaven, that such companions thou'dst unfold,   140
And put in every honest hand a whip
To lash the rascals naked through the world,
Even from the east to th'west!

IAGO   Speak within door.

EMILIA

O fie upon them! Some such squire he was

That turned your wit the seamy side without
And made you to suspect me with the Moor.

IAGO

You are a fool, go to.

DESDEMONA   O good Iago,
What shall I do to win my lord again?
Good friend, go to him; for, by this light of heaven,
150   I know not how I lost him. Here I kneel:
If e'er my will did trespass 'gainst his love,
Either in discourse of thought or actual deed;
Or that mine eyes, mine ears, or any sense
Delighted them in any other form;
Or that I do not yet, and ever did,
And ever will – though he do shake me off
To beggarly divorcement – love him dearly,
Comfort forswear me! Unkindness may do much,
And his unkindness may defeat my life,
160   But never taint my love. I cannot say 'whore':
It does abhor me now I speak the word;
To do the act that might the addition earn
Not the world's mass of vanity could make me.

IAGO

I pray you, be content: 'tis but his humour;
The business of the state does him offence,
And he does chide with you.

DESDEMONA

If 'twere no other –

IAGO   It is so, I warrant.
Hark how these instruments summon to supper!
The messengers of Venice stay the meat.
170   Go in, and weep not; all things shall be well.
                         Exeunt Desdemona and Emilia
        Enter Roderigo
How now, Roderigo?

RODERIGO I do not find that thou deal'st justly with
me.

IAGO What in the contrary?

RODERIGO Every day thou daff'st me with some device,
Iago, and rather, as it seems to me now, keep'st from me
all conveniency, than suppliest me with the least advantage of hope. I will indeed no longer endure it. Nor
am I yet persuaded to put up in peace what already I
have foolishly suffered.   180

IAGO Will you hear me, Roderigo?

RODERIGO Faith, I have heard too much; for your words
and performances are no kin together.

IAGO You charge me most unjustly.

RODERIGO With naught but truth. I have wasted myself
out of my means. The jewels you have had from me to
deliver to Desdemona would half have corrupted a
votarist. You have told me she hath received them, and
returned me expectations and comforts of sudden respect
and acquaintance, but I find none.   190

IAGO Well, go to; very well.

RODERIGO Very well, go to! I cannot go to, man, nor 'tis
not very well. Nay, I think it is scurvy and begin to
find myself fopped in it.

IAGO Very well.

RODERIGO I tell you, 'tis not very well. I will make myself
known to Desdemona. If she will return me my jewels,
I will give over my suit and repent my unlawful solicita-
tion. If not, assure yourself I will seek satisfaction of
you.   200

IAGO You have said now.

RODERIGO Ay, and said nothing but what I protest
intendment of doing.

IAGO Why, now I see there's mettle in thee; and even from
this instant do build on thee a better opinion than ever

before. Give me thy hand, Roderigo. Thou hast taken
against me a most just exception; but yet I protest I have
dealt most directly in thy affair.

RODERIGO It hath not appeared.

210 IAGO I grant indeed it hath not appeared; and your suspicion is not without wit and judgement. But, Roderigo,
if thou hast that in thee indeed, which I have greater
reason to believe now than ever – I mean purpose,
courage, and valour – this night show it. If thou the
next night following enjoy not Desdemona, take me from
this world with treachery, and devise engines for my life.

RODERIGO Well, what is it? Is it within reason and
compass?

IAGO Sir, there is especial commission come from Venice
220 to depute Cassio in Othello's place.

RODERIGO Is that true? Why, then Othello and Desdemona return again to Venice.

IAGO O, no: he goes into Mauritania and takes away with
him the fair Desdemona, unless his abode be lingered
here by some accident: wherein none can be so determinate as the removing of Cassio.

RODERIGO How do you mean 'removing' of him?

IAGO Why, by making him uncapable of Othello's place –
knocking out his brains.

230 RODERIGO And that you would have me to do?

IAGO Ay, if you dare do yourself a profit and a right. He
sups tonight with a harlotry; and thither will I go to
him. He knows not yet of his honourable fortune. If
you will watch his going thence – which I will fashion to
fall out between twelve and one – you may take him at
your pleasure. I will be near to second your attempt,
and he shall fall between us. Come, stand not amazed
at it, but go along with me. I will show you such a
necessity in his death that you shall think yourself

bound to put it on him. It is now high supper-time and   240
the night grows to waste. About it!
RODERIGO I will hear further reason for this.
IAGO And you shall be satisfied.   *Exeunt*

Enter Othello, Lodovico, Desdemona, Emilia, and   IV.3
attendants

LODOVICO
I do beseech you, sir, trouble yourself no further.
OTHELLO
O, pardon me: 'twill do me good to walk.
LODOVICO
Madam, good night. I humbly thank your ladyship.
DESDEMONA
Your honour is most welcome.
OTHELLO   Will you walk, sir?
O, Desdemona!
DESDEMONA
My lord?
OTHELLO Get you to bed on th'instant. I will be returned
forthwith. Dismiss your attendant there. Look't be done.
DESDEMONA I will, my lord.
        Exeunt Othello, Lodovico, and attendants
EMILIA
How goes it now? He looks gentler than he did.   10
DESDEMONA
He says he will return incontinent.
He hath commanded me to go to bed,
And bade me to dismiss you.
EMILIA   Dismiss me?
DESDEMONA
It was his bidding: therefore, good Emilia,

Give me my nightly wearing, and adieu.
We must not now displease him.

EMILIA

I would you had never seen him.

DESDEMONA

So would not I: my love doth so approve him
That even his stubbornness, his checks, his frowns –
Prithee, unpin me – have grace and favour in them.

EMILIA

I have laid those sheets, you bade me, on the bed.

DESDEMONA

All's one. Good faith, how foolish are our minds!
If I do die before thee, prithee shroud me
In one of those same sheets.

EMILIA   Come, come, you talk.

DESDEMONA

My mother had a maid called Barbary:
She was in love: and he she loved proved mad
And did forsake her. She had a song of willow;
An old thing 'twas; but it expressed her fortune,
And she died singing it. That song tonight
Will not go from my mind: I have much to do
But to go hang my head all at one side,
And sing it like poor Barbary – prithee, dispatch.

EMILIA

Shall I go fetch your night-gown?

DESDEMONA   No, unpin me here.
This Lodovico is a proper man.

EMILIA

A very handsome man.

DESDEMONA   He speaks well.

EMILIA I know a lady in Venice would have walked bare-
foot to Palestine for a touch of his nether lip.

DESDEMONA (*sings*)
    The poor soul sat sighing by a sycamore tree,
        Sing all a green willow;
    Her hand on her bosom, her head on her knee,   40
        Sing willow, willow, willow;
    The fresh streams ran by her and murmured her
        moans;
        Sing willow, willow, willow;
    Her salt tears fell from her and softened the stones –
    (*She speaks*)
Lay by these.
    (*She sings*)
        Sing willow, willow, willow –
    (*She speaks*)
Prithee hie thee; he'll come anon.
    (*She sings*)
    Sing all a green willow must be my garland.
    Let nobody blame him; his scorn I approve –
    (*She speaks*)
Nay, that's not next. Hark, who is't that knocks?   50
EMILIA It's the wind.
DESDEMONA (*sings*)
    I called my love false love, but what said he then?
        Sing willow, willow, willow:
    If I court moe women, you'll couch with moe men.
    (*She speaks*)
So get thee gone; good night. Mine eyes do itch:
Does that bode weeping?
EMILIA   'Tis neither here nor there.
DESDEMONA
I have heard it said so. O, these men, these men!
Dost thou in conscience think – tell me, Emilia –
That there be women do abuse their husbands
In such gross kind?

60   EMILIA   There be some such, no question.

DESDEMONA
      Wouldst thou do such a deed for all the world?

EMILIA
      Why, would not you?

DESDEMONA   No, by this heavenly light.

EMILIA Nor I neither by this heavenly light: I might do't
      as well i'th'dark.

DESDEMONA Wouldst thou do such a deed for all the
      world?

EMILIA The world's a huge thing: it is a great price for a
      small vice.

DESDEMONA In troth, I think thou wouldst not.

70   EMILIA In troth I think I should, and undo't when I had
      done it. Marry, I would not do such a thing for a joint
      ring, nor for measures of lawn, nor for gowns, petticoats,
      nor caps, nor any petty exhibition. But for all the whole
      world! Ud's pity, who would not make her husband a
      cuckold, to make him a monarch? I should venture
      purgatory for't.

DESDEMONA Beshrew me, if I would do such a wrong for
      the whole world!

EMILIA Why, the wrong is but a wrong i'th'world; and
80   having the world for your labour, 'tis a wrong in your
      own world, and you might quickly make it right.

DESDEMONA I do not think there is any such woman.

EMILIA Yes, a dozen: and as many to th'vantage as would
      store the world they played for.
      But I do think it is their husbands' faults
      If wives do fall. Say that they slack their duties,
      And pour our treasures into foreign laps;
      Or else break out in peevish jealousies,
      Throwing restraint upon us; or say they strike us,
90   Or scant our former having in despite –

Why, we have galls, and though we have some grace,
Yet have we some revenge. Let husbands know
Their wives have sense like them: they see and smell,
And have their palates both for sweet and sour
As husbands have. What is it that they do,
When they change us for others? Is it sport?
I think it is. And doth affection breed it?
I think it doth. Is't frailty that thus errs?
It is so too. And have not we affections,
Desires for sport, and frailty, as men have?   100
Then let them use us well: else let them know
The ills we do, their ills instruct us so.

DESDEMONA
Good night, good night. God me such uses send,
Not to pick bad from bad, but by bad mend! *Exeunt*

                                    *

                    Enter Iago and Roderigo   V. I
IAGO
Here, stand behind this bulk: straight will he come.
Wear thy good rapier bare, and put it home.
Quick, quick; fear nothing: I'll be at thy elbow.
It makes us, or it mars us; think on that,
And fix most firm thy resolution.
RODERIGO
Be near at hand; I may miscarry in't.
IAGO
Here, at thy hand: be bold, and take thy stand.
                                    He retires

RODERIGO
I have no great devotion to the deed,
And yet he hath given me satisfying reasons.

10   'Tis but a man gone. Forth my sword! He dies!

IAGO
      I have rubbed this young quat almost to the sense,
      And he grows angry. Now, whether he kill Cassio,
      Or Cassio him, or each do kill the other,
      Every way makes my gain. Live Roderigo,
      He calls me to a restitution large
      Of gold and jewels, that I bobbed from him
      As gifts to Desdemona.
      It must not be. If Cassio do remain
      He hath a daily beauty in his life
20   That makes me ugly: and besides, the Moor
      May unfold me to him – there stand I in much peril.
      No, he must die. But soft, I hear him coming.
          Enter Cassio

RODERIGO
      I know his gait; 'tis he. Villain, thou diest!

CASSIO
      That thrust had been mine enemy indeed,
      But that my coat is better than thou think'st.
      I will make proof of thine.
          He wounds Roderigo

RODERIGO   O, I am slain!
                    Iago wounds Cassio in the leg, and exit

CASSIO
      I am maimed for ever. Help, ho! Murder, murder!
          Enter Othello, above

OTHELLO
      The voice of Cassio: Iago keeps his word.

RODERIGO
      O, villain that I am!

OTHELLO   It is even so.

CASSIO
30   O, help, ho! Light! A surgeon!

OTHELLO

'Tis he! O brave Iago, honest and just,
That hast such noble sense of thy friend's wrong,
Thou teachest me! Minion, your dear lies dead,
And your unblest fate hies. Strumpet, I come!
Forth of my heart those charms, thine eyes, are blotted;
Thy bed, lust-stained, shall with lust's blood be spotted.

Exit Othello

Enter Lodovico and Gratiano

CASSIO

What, ho! No watch? No passage? Murder, murder!

GRATIANO

'Tis some mischance: the cry is very direful.

CASSIO

O, help!

LODOVICO

Hark!   40

RODERIGO

O wretched villain!

LODOVICO

Two or three groan. It is a heavy night.
These may be counterfeits. Let's think't unsafe
To come in to the cry without more help.

RODERIGO

Nobody come? Then shall I bleed to death.

LODOVICO

Hark!

Enter Iago, with a light

GRATIANO

Here's one comes in his shirt, with light and weapons.

IAGO

Who's there? Whose noise is this that cries on murder?

LODOVICO

We do not know.

IAGO   Did you not hear a cry?
CASSIO
50   Here, here: for heaven's sake help me!
IAGO   What's the matter?
GRATIANO
    This is Othello's Ancient, as I take it.
LODOVICO
    The same indeed, a very valiant fellow.
IAGO
    What are you here, that cry so grievously?
CASSIO
    Iago? O, I am spoiled, undone by villains!
    Give me some help.
IAGO
    O me, Lieutenant! What villains have done this?
CASSIO
    I think that one of them is hereabout
    And cannot make away.
IAGO   O treacherous villains!
    What are you there? Come in, and give some help.
RODERIGO
60   O, help me here!
CASSIO
    That's one of them.
IAGO   O murd'rous slave! O villain!
        He stabs Roderigo
RODERIGO
    O damned Iago! O inhuman dog!
        He faints
IAGO
    Kill men i'th'dark? Where be these bloody thieves?
    How silent is this town! Ho, murder, murder!
        Lodovico and Gratiano come forward
    What may you be? Are you of good or evil?

LODOVICO

As you shall prove us, praise us.

IAGO

Signor Lodovico?

LODOVICO

He, sir.

IAGO

I cry you mercy. Here's Cassio hurt by villains.

GRATIANO

Cassio?   70

IAGO

How is't, brother?

CASSIO

My leg is cut in two.

IAGO   Marry, heaven forbid!

Light, gentlemen. I'll bind it with my shirt.

   Enter Bianca

BIANCA

What is the matter, ho? Who is't that cried?

IAGO

Who is't that cried?

BIANCA

O, my dear Cassio, my sweet Cassio,

O Cassio, Cassio, Cassio!

IAGO

O notable strumpet! Cassio, may you suspect

Who they should be that have thus mangled you?

CASSIO

No.   80

GRATIANO

I am sorry to find you thus: I have been to seek you.

IAGO

Lend me a garter: so. O, for a chair

To bear him easily hence!

BIANCA   Alas, he faints!
  O Cassio, Cassio, Cassio!

IAGO
  Gentlemen all, I do suspect this trash
  To be a party in this injury.
  Patience awhile, good Cassio. Come, come,
  Lend me a light. Know we this face or no?
  Alas, my friend, and my dear countryman
90 Roderigo? No – yes, sure – O heaven, Roderigo!

GRATIANO
  What! Of Venice?

IAGO
  Even he, sir. Did you know him?

GRATIANO   Know him? Ay.

IAGO
  Signor Gratiano? I cry you gentle pardon.
  These bloody accidents must excuse my manners
  That so neglected you.

GRATIANO   I am glad to see you.

IAGO
  How do you, Cassio? O, a chair, a chair!

GRATIANO
  Roderigo!

IAGO
  He, he, 'tis he.

Enter attendants with chair

          O, that's well said, the chair!
  Some good man bear him carefully from hence.
100 I'll fetch the General's surgeon. For you, mistress,
  Save you your labour. He that lies slain here, Cassio,
  Was my dear friend. What malice was between you?

CASSIO
  None in the world, nor do I know the man.

IAGO

(*to Bianca*) What, look you pale? O, bear him out
    o'th'air.

> *Cassio is borne in. Roderigo's body is removed*

Stay you, good gentlemen. Look you pale, mistress?
Do you perceive the gastness of her eye?
Nay, if you stare, we shall hear more anon.
Behold her well; I pray you look upon her.
Do you see, gentlemen? Nay, guiltiness will speak
Though tongues were out of use.   110

> *Enter Emilia*

EMILIA

'Las, what's the matter? What's the matter, husband?

IAGO

Cassio hath here been set on in the dark
By Roderigo and fellows that are scaped:
He's almost slain and Roderigo quite.

EMILIA

Alas, good gentleman! Alas, good Cassio!

IAGO

This is the fruit of whoring. Prithee, Emilia,
Go know of Cassio where he supped tonight.
What, do you shake at that?

BIANCA

He supped at my house, but I therefore shake not.

IAGO

O, did he so? I charge you go with me.   120

EMILIA

O, fie upon thee, strumpet!

BIANCA

I am no strumpet, but of life as honest
As you that thus abuse me.

EMILIA   As I? Foh! Fie upon thee!

IAGO

    Kind gentlemen, let's see poor Cassio dressed.
    Come, mistress, you must tell's another tale.
    Emilia, run you to the citadel,
    And tell my lord and lady what hath happed.
    Will you go on afore? (*Aside*) This is the night
    That either makes me, or fordoes me quite.   *Exeunt*

V.2   *Enter Othello, with a light, Desdemona in her bed*

OTHELLO

    It is the cause, it is the cause, my soul:
    Let me not name it to you, you chaste stars!
    It is the cause. Yet I'll not shed her blood,
    Nor scar that whiter skin of hers than snow,
    And smooth as monumental alabaster:
    Yet she must die, else she'll betray more men.
    Put out the light, and then put out the light:
    If I quench thee, thou flaming minister,
    I can again thy former light restore,
10   Should I repent me; but once put out thy light,
    Thou cunning'st pattern of excelling nature,
    I know not where is that Promethean heat
    That can thy light relume. When I have plucked thy rose,
    I cannot give it vital growth again,
    It needs must wither. I'll smell it on the tree.
      He kisses her
    O balmy breath, that dost almost persuade
    Justice to break her sword! One more, one more.
    Be thus when thou art dead and I will kill thee,
    And love thee after. One more, and this the last.
20   So sweet was ne'er so fatal. I must weep.
    But they are cruel tears: this sorrow's heavenly –
    It strikes where it doth love. She wakes.

DESDEMONA
Who's there? Othello?

OTHELLO
Ay, Desdemona.

DESDEMONA   Will you come to bed, my lord?

OTHELLO
Have you prayed tonight, Desdemon?

DESDEMONA   Ay, my lord.

OTHELLO
If you bethink yourself of any crime
Unreconciled as yet to heaven and grace,
Solicit for it straight.

DESDEMONA
Alack, my lord, what may you mean by that?

OTHELLO
Well, do it, and be brief; I will walk by: 30
I would not kill thy unprepared spirit;
No – heaven forfend! – I would not kill thy soul.

DESDEMONA
Talk you of killing?

OTHELLO   Ay, I do.

DESDEMONA   Then heaven
Have mercy on me!

OTHELLO   Amen, with all my heart!

DESDEMONA
If you say so, I hope you will not kill me.

OTHELLO
Hum!

DESDEMONA
And yet I fear you: for you're fatal then
When your eyes roll so. Why I should fear I know not,
Since guiltiness I know not; but yet I feel I fear.

OTHELLO
Think on thy sins.

40 DESDEMONA   They are loves I bear to you.
    OTHELLO
    Ay, and for that thou diest.
    DESDEMONA
    That death's unnatural that kills for loving.
    Alas, why gnaw you so your nether lip?
    Some bloody passion shakes your very frame:
    These are portènts; but yet I hope, I hope
    They do not point on me.
    OTHELLO   Peace, and be still!
    DESDEMONA
    I will – so. What's the matter?
    OTHELLO
    That handkerchief which I so loved and gave thee,
    Thou gav'st to Cassio.
    DESDEMONA   No, by my life and soul!
50 Send for the man and ask him.
    OTHELLO   Sweet soul, take heed,
    Take heed of perjury: thou art on thy death-bed.
    DESDEMONA
    Ay, but not yet to die.
    OTHELLO   Yes, presently.
    Therefore confess thee freely of thy sin;
    For to deny each article with oath
    Cannot remove nor choke the strong conception
    That I do groan withal. Thou art to die.
    DESDEMONA
    Then Lord have mercy on me!
    OTHELLO   I say, amen.
    DESDEMONA
    And have you mercy too! I never did
    Offend you in my life; never loved Cassio
60 But with such general warranty of heaven
    As I might love. I never gave him token.

OTHELLO
  By heaven, I saw my handkerchief in's hand!
  O perjured woman! Thou dost stone my heart,
  And mak'st me call what I intend to do
  A murder, which I thought a sacrifice.
  I saw the handkerchief.
DESDEMONA   He found it then.
  I never gave it him. Send for him hither.
  Let him confess a truth.
OTHELLO   He hath confessed.
DESDEMONA
  What, my lord?
OTHELLO
  That he hath used thee.
DESDEMONA   How? Unlawfully?   70
OTHELLO
  Ay.
DESDEMONA
  He will not say so.
OTHELLO   No, his mouth is stopped:
  Honest Iago hath ta'en order for't.
DESDEMONA
  O, my fear interprets! What, is he dead?
OTHELLO
  Had all his hairs been lives, my great revenge
  Had stomach for them all.
DESDEMONA
  Alas, he is betrayed, and I undone.
OTHELLO
  Out, strumpet! Weep'st thou for him to my face?
DESDEMONA
  O banish me, my lord, but kill me not!
OTHELLO
  Down, strumpet!   80

DESDEMONA

Kill me tomorrow: let me live tonight!

OTHELLO

Nay, if you strive —

DESDEMONA

But half an hour!

OTHELLO   Being done, there is no pause.

DESDEMONA

But while I say one prayer!

OTHELLO   It is too late.

DESDEMONA

O Lord, Lord, Lord!

He smothers her

EMILIA

(*without*) My lord, my lord! What, ho! My lord, my lord!

OTHELLO

What noise is this? Not dead? Not yet quite dead?
I, that am cruel, am yet merciful:
I would not have thee linger in thy pain.
90   So, so.

EMILIA (*without*) What, ho! My lord, my lord!

OTHELLO   Who's there?

EMILIA

(*without*) O, good my lord, I'd speak a word with you.

OTHELLO

Yes, 'tis Emilia. — By and by. — She's dead.
'Tis like she comes to speak of Cassio's death:
The noise was high. Ha! No more moving?
Still as the grave. Shall she come in? Were't good?
I think she stirs again. No. What's best to do?
If she come in, she'll sure speak to my wife —
My wife! My wife! What wife? I have no wife.
O, insupportable! O heavy hour!
100   Methinks it should be now a huge eclipse

Of sun and moon, and that th'affrighted globe
Should yawn at alteration.
EMILIA   I do beseech you
That I may speak with you. O, good my lord!
OTHELLO
I had forgot thee. O, come in, Emilia.
Soft; by and by. Let me the curtains draw.
Where art thou? (*He unlocks door*) What's the matter
    with thee now?
    Enter Emilia
EMILIA
O, my good lord, yonder's foul murder done.
OTHELLO
What! Now?
EMILIA
But now, my lord.
OTHELLO
It is the very error of the moon;   110
She comes more nearer earth than she was wont,
And makes men mad.
EMILIA
    Cassio, my lord, hath killed a young Venetian
Called Roderigo.
OTHELLO   Roderigo killed?
And Cassio killed?
EMILIA   No, Cassio is not killed.
OTHELLO
Not Cassio killed! Then murder's out of tune,
And sweet revenge grows harsh.
DESDEMONA
    O, falsely, falsely murdered!
EMILIA   O Lord! What cry is that?
OTHELLO
That? What?

EMILIA

120   Out and alas, that was my lady's voice!
         She draws back the curtains
       Help, help, ho, help! O, lady, speak again!
       Sweet Desdemona, O sweet mistress, speak!

DESDEMONA

       A guiltless death I die.

EMILIA

       O, who hath done this deed?

DESDEMONA

       Nobody – I myself – farewell.
       Commend me to my kind lord – O, farewell! *She dies*

OTHELLO

       Why, how should she be murdered?

EMILIA   Alas, who knows?

OTHELLO

       You heard her say herself it was not I.

EMILIA

       She said so: I must needs report the truth.

OTHELLO

130   She's like a liar gone to burning hell:
       'Twas I that killed her.

EMILIA   O, the more angel she,
       And you the blacker devil!

OTHELLO

       She turned to folly; and she was a whore.

EMILIA

       Thou dost belie her, and thou art a devil.

OTHELLO

       She was false as water.

EMILIA   Thou art rash as fire to say
       That she was false. O, she was heavenly true!

OTHELLO

       Cassio did top her: ask thy husband else.

O, I were damned beneath all depth in hell
But that I did proceed upon just grounds
To this extremity. Thy husband knew it all.   140

EMILIA
My husband!

OTHELLO   Thy husband.

EMILIA   That she was false to wedlock?

OTHELLO
Ay, with Cassio. Nay, had she been true,
If heaven would make me such another world
Of one entire and perfect chrysolite,
I'd not have sold her for it.

EMILIA   My husband!

OTHELLO
Ay, 'twas he that told me on her first.
An honest man he is, and hates the slime
That sticks on filthy deeds.

EMILIA   My husband!

OTHELLO
What needs this iterance, woman? I say thy husband.

EMILIA
O mistress, villainy hath made mocks with love!   150
My husband say that she was false?

OTHELLO   He, woman;
I say thy husband; dost understand the word?
My friend, thy husband, honest, honest Iago.

EMILIA
If he say so, may his pernicious soul
Rot half a grain a day! He lies to th'heart.
She was too fond of her most filthy bargain.

OTHELLO
Ha!

EMILIA
Do thy worst:

This deed of thine is no more worthy heaven
160   Than thou wast worthy her.
OTHELLO   Peace, you were best.
EMILIA
    Thou hast not half that power to do me harm
    As I have to be hurt. O gull! O dolt!
    As ignorant as dirt! Thou hast done a deed –
    I care not for thy sword – I'll make thee known,
    Though I lost twenty lives. Help! Help, ho! Help!
    The Moor hath killed my mistress! Murder! Murder!
        Enter Montano, Gratiano, and Iago
MONTANO
    What is the matter? How now, General?
EMILIA
    O, are you come, Iago? You have done well,
    That men must lay their murders on your neck.
GRATIANO
170   What is the matter?
EMILIA
    Disprove this villain, if thou be'st a man:
    He says thou told'st him that his wife was false.
    I know thou didst not: thou'rt not such a villain.
    Speak, for my heart is full.
IAGO
    I told him what I thought, and told no more
    Than what he found himself was apt and true.
EMILIA
    But did you ever tell him she was false?
IAGO
    I did.
EMILIA
    You told a lie, an odious damnèd lie:
180   Upon my soul, a lie, a wicked lie!
    She false with Cassio! Did you say with Cassio?

IAGO

> With Cassio, mistress! Go to, charm your tongue.

EMILIA

> I will not charm my tongue; I am bound to speak:
> My mistress here lies murdered in her bed.

ALL

> O heavens forfend!

EMILIA

> And your reports have set the murder on.

OTHELLO

> Nay, stare not masters: it is true indeed.

GRATIANO

> 'Tis a strange truth.

MONTANO

> O monstrous act!

EMILIA   Villainy, villainy, villainy!

> I think upon't, I think – I smell't – O villainy!   190
> I thought so then; I'll kill myself for grief.
> O villainy, villainy!

IAGO

> What, are you mad? I charge you get you home.

EMILIA

> Good gentlemen, let me have leave to speak.
> 'Tis proper I obey him, but not now.
> Perchance, Iago, I will ne'er go home.

OTHELLO

> (*falling on bed*) O! O! O!

EMILIA   Nay, lay thee down and roar,

> For thou hast killed the sweetest innocent
> That e'er did lift up eye.

OTHELLO (*rising*)   O, she was foul!

> I scarce did know you, uncle; there lies your niece,   200
> Whose breath indeed these hands have newly stopped.
> I know this act shows horrible and grim.

GRATIANO

    Poor Desdemon, I am glad thy father's dead:
    Thy match was mortal to him, and pure grief
    Shore his old thread in twain. Did he live now,
    This sight would make him do a desperate turn,
    Yea, curse his better angel from his side,
    And fall to reprobance.

OTHELLO

    'Tis pitiful: but yet Iago knows
210   That she with Cassio hath the act of shame
    A thousand times committed. Cassio confessed it,
    And she did gratify his amorous works
    With that recognizance and pledge of love
    Which I first gave her. I saw it in his hand:
    It was a handkerchief, an antique token
    My father gave my mother.

EMILIA   O God! O heavenly Powers!

IAGO

    Zounds, hold your peace!

EMILIA   'Twill out, 'twill out. I peace?
    No, I will speak as liberal as the north;
    Let heaven, and men, and devils, let them all,
220   All, all cry shame against me, yet I'll speak.

IAGO

    Be wise, and get you home.

EMILIA   I will not.

    Iago draws his sword

GRATIANO   Fie!
    Your sword upon a woman!

EMILIA

    O thou dull Moor, that handkerchief thou speak'st of
    I found by fortune and did give my husband,
    For often, with a solemn earnestness –
    More than indeed belonged to such a trifle –

He begged of me to steal it.

IAGO   Villainous whore!

EMILIA

She give it Cassio? No, alas, I found it
And I did give't my husband.

IAGO   Filth, thou liest!

EMILIA

By heaven I do not, I do not, gentlemen.   230
O murderous coxcomb, what should such a fool
Do with so good a wife?

OTHELLO   Are there no stones in heaven
But what serve for the thunder? Precious villain!

> *He runs at Iago: Montano disarms him;*
> *Iago stabs Emilia from behind and exit*

GRATIANO

The woman falls: sure he hath killed his wife.

EMILIA

Ay, ay: O, lay me by my mistress' side.

GRATIANO

He's gone, but his wife's killed.

MONTANO

'Tis a notorious villain. Take you this weapon,
Which I have here recovered from the Moor.
Come guard the door without: let him not pass,
But kill him rather. I'll after that same villain,   240
For 'tis a damnèd slave.

> *Exeunt Montano and Gratiano*

OTHELLO   I am not valiant neither,
But every puny whipster gets my sword.
But why should honour outlive honesty?
Let it go all.

EMILIA   What did thy song bode, lady?
Hark, canst thou hear me? I will play the swan
And die in music. (*Singing*) Willow, willow, willow.

Moor, she was chaste; she loved thee, cruel Moor,
So come my soul to bliss, as I speak true;
So speaking as I think, I die, I die.   *She dies*

OTHELLO

250   I have another weapon in this chamber:
It was a sword of Spain, the ice-brook's temper.
O, here it is. Uncle, I must come forth.

GRATIANO

(*within*) If thou attempt it, it will cost thee dear;
Thou hast no weapon, and perforce must suffer.

OTHELLO

Look in upon me then, and speak with me,
Or naked as I am I will assault thee.
      Enter Gratiano

GRATIANO

What is the matter?

OTHELLO   Behold, I have a weapon:
A better never did itself sustain
Upon a soldier's thigh. I have seen the day

260   That with this little arm and this good sword,
I have made my way through more impediments
Than twenty times your stop. But, O vain boast! –
Who can control his fate? – 'Tis not so now.
Be not afraid, though you do see me weaponed:
Here is my journey's end, here is my butt
And very sea-mark of my utmost sail.
Do you go back dismayed? 'Tis a lost fear:
Man but a rush against Othello's breast,
And he retires. Where should Othello go?
      He goes to the bed

270   Now, how dost thou look now? O ill-starred wench
Pale as thy smock! When we shall meet at compt
This look of thine will hurl my soul from heaven
And fiends will snatch at it. Cold, cold, my girl,

Even like thy chastity.
O cursèd, cursèd slave! Whip me, ye devils,
From the possession of this heavenly sight!
Blow me about in winds! Roast me in sulphur!
Wash me in steep-down gulfs of liquid fire!
O Desdemon! Dead Desdemon! Dead! O! O!

*Enter Lodovico, Cassio in a chair, Montano and Iago
with Officers*

LODOVICO
Where is this rash and most unfortunate man?   280
OTHELLO
That's he that was Othello: here I am.
LODOVICO
Where is that viper? Bring the villain forth.
OTHELLO
I look down towards his feet; but that's a fable.
If that thou be'st a devil, I cannot kill thee.

He wounds Iago

LODOVICO
Wrench his sword from him.
IAGO   I bleed, sir, but not killed.
OTHELLO
I am not sorry neither; I'd have thee live,
For in my sense 'tis happiness to die.
LODOVICO
O, thou Othello, that wast once so good,
Fallen in the practice of a damnèd slave,
What shall be said to thee?
OTHELLO   Why, anything: 290
An honourable murderer, if you will:
For naught did I in hate, but all in honour.
LODOVICO
This wretch hath part confessed his villainy.
Did you and he consent in Cassio's death?

OTHELLO
  Ay.
CASSIO
  Dear General, I never gave you cause.
OTHELLO
  I do believe it, and I ask your pardon.
  Will you, I pray, demand that demi-devil
  Why he hath thus ensnared my soul and body?
IAGO
300 Demand me nothing; what you know, you know:
  From this time forth I never will speak word.
LODOVICO
  What! Not to pray?
GRATIANO
  Torments will ope your lips.
OTHELLO   Well, thou dost best.
LODOVICO
  Sir, you shall understand what hath befallen,
  Which, as I think, you know not. Here is a letter
  Found in the pocket of the slain Roderigo,
  And here another: the one of them imports
  The death of Cassio, to be undertook
  By Roderigo.
OTHELLO   O villain!
CASSIO   Most heathenish and most gross!
LODOVICO
310 Now here's another discontented paper
  Found in his pocket too; and this, it seems
  Roderigo meant to have sent this damnèd villain,
  But that, belike, Iago, in the nick,
  Came in and satisfied him.
OTHELLO   O the pernicious caitiff!
  How came you, Cassio, by that handkerchief
  That was my wife's?

CASSIO   I found it in my chamber;
  And he himself confessed but even now
  That there he dropped it for a special purpose
  Which wrought to his desire.
OTHELLO   O fool, fool, fool!
CASSIO
  There is besides, in Roderigo's letter,   320
  How he upbraids Iago, that he made him
  Brave me upon the watch, whereon it came
  That I was cast; and even but now he spake
  After long seeming dead – Iago hurt him,
  Iago set him on.
LODOVICO
  You must forsake this room and go with us.
  Your power and your command is taken off
  And Cassio rules in Cyprus. For this slave,
  If there be any cunning cruelty
  That can torment him much, and hold him long,   330
  It shall be his. You shall close prisoner rest,
  Till that the nature of your fault be known
  To the Venetian state. Come, bring him away.
OTHELLO
  Soft you; a word or two before you go.
  I have done the state some service and they know't:
  No more of that. I pray you in your letters
  When you shall these unlucky deeds relate
  Speak of me as I am: nothing extenuate,
  Nor set down aught in malice. Then must you speak
  Of one that loved not wisely, but too well;   340
  Of one, not easily jealous but, being wrought,
  Perplexed in the extreme; of one whose hand
  Like the base Indian threw a pearl away
  Richer than all his tribe; of one whose sùbdued eyes,
  Albeit unusèd to the melting mood,

Drop tears as fast as the Arabian trees
Their med'cinable gum. Set you down this:
And say, besides, that in Aleppo once
Where a malignant and a turbaned Turk
350 Beat a Venetian and traduced the state,
I took by th'throat the circumcisèd dog
And smote him thus.

He stabs himself

LODOVICO

O bloody period!

GRATIANO   All that's spoke is marred!

OTHELLO

I kissed thee, ere I killed thee: no way but this,
Killing myself, to die upon a kiss.

He falls on the bed and dies

CASSIO

This did I fear, but thought he had no weapon,
For he was great of heart.

LODOVICO   O, Spartan dog,
More fell than anguish, hunger, or the sea,
Look on the tragic loading of this bed:
360 This is thy work. The object poisons sight:
Let it be hid.

The curtains are drawn

                    Gratiano, keep the house
And seize upon the fortunes of the Moor,
For they succeed on you. To you, Lord Governor,
Remains the censure of this hellish villain:
The time, the place, the torture, O, enforce it!
Myself will straight aboard, and to the state
This heavy act with heavy heart relate.   *Exeunt*

An Account of the Text

Othello was first published in 1622, some eighteen years after its first performance, in an edition known as the Quarto (Q). In the following year the play was included in the first Folio (F), the collected edition of Shakespeare's plays. The F text was based partly on that of Q (or on the transcript from which it was printed) and partly on a copy of the prompt book. As both Q and F omit passages, a modern editor has to make use of both. What things caused the divergences are still a matter of debate. Omissions in Q may be due to the transcriber or the compositors, and some of them may rather be due to revisions of the original play (see Coghill below). Omissions in F include the deletion of many oaths in order to comply with the new regulations about profanity; others may be due to the carelessness of the book-keeper who had the job of collating the manuscript with the prompt book. It was probably a rushed job. As some mistakes are common to Q and F, there may well be others impossible to detect.

We may agree with Alice Walker's attack on the Q text (*Shakespeare Survey 5*, 1952; *Textual Problems of the First Folio*, 1953; and her edition of the play, 1957) but she exaggerates its faults, blaming them on the book-keeper 'who saved himself time and trouble by using his memory rather than his eyes'. Nevill Coghill in *Shakespeare's Professional Skills* (1964) argues convincingly that the poet revised the play so as to eliminate weaknesses which had struck him in performance. Roderigo's speech (I.1.123 ff.) clarifies the situation for the audience; the Pontic Sea simile enormously increases the effectiveness of the temptation scene – but this might well be due to careless omission by the transcriber; there are several passages inserted to arouse sympathy for Emilia (e.g. IV.3.85–102). In *The Stability of Shakespeare's Text* (1965) E. A. J. Honigmann argued that Shakespeare, like other poets, introduced variants while copying out his own work; and in a later article in *The Library* (June 1982), without abandoning this theory, he agreed with Coghill that Shakespeare deliberately revised the play. This hypothesis is acted upon by the editors of the Oxford *Complete Works* (1986) and is discussed in *William Shakespeare: A Textual Companion* (by Stanley Wells, Gary Taylor, et al., 1987).

In my own article on the text of *Othello*, written while I was working on this edition, and published in *Shakespeare Studies I* (1965), I argued that although an editor should use F as his copytext, there are scores of Q readings which are manifestly superior, and that it is necessary to deviate from F in approximately 300 places, and that in 200 of them Q should be accepted. When both Q and F are unsatisfactory it is necessary to amend. Every variant must be judged on its merits rather than on the assumption that we should wherever possible follow F. The collations that follow show how much these principles have been applied. The original spellings have been used in these collations.

COLLATIONS

1 Passages Omitted in Quarto

I.1
   122–38 If 't . . . yourself
I.2
      20 Which, when I know
      65 If . . . bound
   72–7 Judge . . . attach thee
I.3
      16 By Signor Angelo
  24–30 For . . . profitless
      63 Being . . . sense
   118 The . . . you
   123 I . . . blood
   192 Which . . . heart

273 her
274 it
280 So
308 O villainous
345–6 She must change for youth
357–8 if . . . issue
376 I'll sell all my land

II.1

39–40 Even . . . regard
63 quirks of
112 DESDEMONA
154 See . . . behind
234 Why, none; why, none
237–8 a devilish knave
246 Blessed pudding
248 that I did
249 obscure
252 Villainous thoughts, Roderigo
254 master and
255 Pish

II.2

9 of feasting

II.3

67 O
96 to be
98–9 and . . . saved
112 Why
184 to
245 dear
297 O, strange

III.1

54 CASSIO I am much bound to you

III.3

163 OTHELLO Ha
380–87 By . . . satisfied
450–57 Iago . . . heaven
465 in me

III.4

8–10 CLOWN To . . . this

      98 of it
    179 Well, well
  191–2 BIANCA ... not
IV.1
  37–43 To ... devil
    120 What! A customer
    123 they
 174–6 IAGO Yours ... whore
    179 that
IV.2
    50 utmost
  72–5 Committed ... committed
   185 With naught but truth
   217 what is it
IV.3
  30–50 I have ... next
  57–60 I ... question
 85–102 But ... so
V.1
    21 much
V.2
    83 OTHELLO Being ... pause
 150–53 EMILIA ... Iago
 184–92 My ... villainy
 244–6 EMILIA What ... willow
 264–70 Be ... wench
   334 before you go

2 Passages Omitted in Folio

I.1
    1 Tush
    4 'Sblood (*later examples of oaths are not listed*)
   15 And in conclusion
  117 now
I.3
  106 DUKE
  199 Into your favour

274 You must hence tonight
372–5 RODERIGO ... purse
II.1
82 And ... comfort
88 me
116 thou (*after* wouldst)
264 with his truncheon
II.3
322 here
III.1
29 CASSIO Do ... friend
48 To ... front
III.3
178 once
183 well
221 at
421 then
449 perhaps
III.4
22 of
37 yet
84 sir
90 OTHELLO ... Cassio
IV.1
52 No, forbear
103 now
110 a
120 her
124 shall
135–6 by this hand
248 an
IV.2
32 But not the words
80 Impudent strumpet
166 And ... you
187 to
227 of

IV.3

 20 in them
 23 thee
 71 it

V.2

 52 Yes
 85 DESDEMONA O Lord, Lord, Lord
 143 Nay
 238 here
 333 him

3 Readings Accepted from Quarto, with Rejected Folio Reading

I.1

 25 togèd] Tongued
 30 Christian] Christen'd
 67 full] fall
  thick-lips] Thicks-lips
 101 bravery] knauerie
 104 them] their
 147 produced] producted
 183 night] might

I.2

 10 pray] pray you
 15 and] or
 16 That] The
 21 provulgate] promulgate
 68 darlings] Deareling
 84 Where] Whether

I.3

 1 these] this
 4 and forty] forty
 35 injointed] inioynted them
 45 wish] to
 93 proceedings] proceeding
 99 maimed] main'd
 107 overt] ouer
 122 till] tell

129 fortunes] Fortune
138 travels'] Trauellours
140 and hills] Hills
heads] head
141 the] my
142 other] others
144 Do grow] Grew
This] These things
146 thence] hence
154 intentively] instinctiuely
158 sighs] kisses
182 lord of all my] the Lord of
217 ear] eares
237–8 If . . . father's.] Why at her Fathers?
239 Nor I: I would not] Nor would I
244 you? Speak.] you Desdemona?
245 did love] loue
254 which] why
265 For] When
267 instruments] Instrument
274–5 You . . . night] *Sen.* You must away to night
279 With] And
296 matters] matter
306 we have] haue we
310 a man] man
327 our (*after* stings)] or
338–9 be . . . continue] be long that Desdemona should
continue
345 acerbe as the] bitter as
347 error] errors
389 ear] eares

II.1

11 banning] foaming
19 they] to
33 prays] praye
34 heaven] Heauens
42 arrivance] Arriuancie
43 this] the
70 clog] enclogge

92 the sea] sea
94 their] this
104 list] leaue
155 wight] wightes
171 an] and
208 hither] thither
217–18 And will she] To
221 again] a game
230 eminently] eminent
235 finder out of occasions] finder of occasion
236 has] he's
253 mutualities] mutabilities
290 for wife] for wift
297 rank] right

II.3

37 unfortunate] infortunate
75 expert] exquisite
124 the prologue] his prologue
152 God's will] Alas
156 God's ... hold] Fie, fie Lieutenant
157 You will be shamed] You'le be asham'd
159 death] death. He dies
227 the] then
234 can I not] cannot I
259 thought] had thought
265 ways] more wayes
292 not so] not
305 I'll] I
344 fortunes] Fortune
352 enmesh] en-mash
367 By th'mass] Introth
374 the while] a while

III.1

21 hear] heare me

III.3

4 case] cause
16 circumstance] Circumstances
39 sneak] steale
60 or] on

66 their] her
74 By'r Lady] Trust me
105 By . . . me] Alas, thou ecchos't me
106 his] thy
111 In] Of
134 free to] free
137 a breast] that breast
138 But some] Wherein
139 session] Sessions
148 conjects] conceits
180 blown] blow'd
196 eye] eyes
200 God] Heauen
213 In faith] Trust me
215 my] your
231 disproportion] disproportions
246 to hold him] to him
256 qualities] Quantities
270 of] to
274 Desdemona] Look where she
275 O . . . mocks] Heauen mock'd
299 A] You haue a
308 faith] but
335 of] in
337 well] well, fed well
370 defend] forgiue
383 Her] My
390 I] and I
392 supervisor] super-vision
422 Over . . . sighed . . . kissed] ore . . . sigh . . . kisse
423 Cried] cry
426 'Tis . . . dream] *Given to Othello*
429 but] yet
444 thy hollow cell] the hollow hell

III.4

5 one] me
  is] 'tis
23 that] the
54 faith . . . That is] indeed . . . That's

64 wive] Wiu'd
67 lose] loose't
94 I'faith] Insooth
95 Zounds] Away
133 can he be] is he
143 that] a
159 that] the
167 I'faith] Indeed
183 by my faith] in good troth
184 sweet] neither

IV.1

9 So] If
21 infected] infectious
37 confession] Confessions
45 , work] workes
60 No] not
77 unsuiting] resulting F; vnfitting Q (*uncorrected state*)
79 scuse] scuses
98 refrain] restraine
107 power] dowre
111 i'faith] indeed
124 Faith] Why
131 beckons] becomes
139 hales] shakes
152 not know] know not
162 street] streets
191 a thousand, thousand times] a thousand, a thousand
    times
214 Come . . . him] this, comes from the Duke. See,
    your wife's with him
216 Senators] the Senators
238 By my troth] Trust me
278 this] his
281 denote] deonte

IV.2

23 Pray] Pray you
29 Nay] May
30 knees] knee

54 unmoving] and mouing
91 keep] keepes
116 As ... bear] That ... beare it
125 all] and
140 heaven] Heauens
147 O good] Alas
154 in] or
169 stay] staies
223 takes] taketh

IV.3

12 He] And
17 I would] I, would
22 faith] Father
24 those] these
74 Ud's pity] why

V.1

1 bulk] Barke
25 think'st] know'st
35 Forth] For
38 cry] voyce
42 It is a] 'Tis
49 Did] Do
50 heaven's] heauen
60 here] there
90 O heaven] Yes, 'tis
93 you] your
104 out o'th'] o'th'
111 'Las ... What's] Alas, what is ... what is
116 fruit] fruits
123 Foh! Fie] Fie

V.2

15 it] thee
19 this] that's
32 heaven] Heauens
35 say so] say
57 Then Lord] O Heauen
102 Should] Did
118 O Lord] Alas

151 that she] she
227 steal it] steal't
249 I die, I die] alas, I dye
289 damnèd] cursed
292 did I] I did
312 to have] t'haue
313 nick] interim
314 the] thou
317 but] it but
343 Indian] Iudean

4 Some Rejected Quarto Variants

1.1

33 Moorship's] Worships
39 affined] assign'd
66 daws] Doues
73 chances ... on't] changes ... out
141 thus deluding you] this delusion
146 place] pate
166 she deceives] thou deceiuest
173 maidhood] manhood

1.2

22 siege] height
41 sequent] frequent
46 hath sent about] sent aboue

1.3

6 the aim] they aym'd
122 truly] faithfull
138 portance in] with it all
165 hint] heate
175 on my head] lite on me
246 storm] scorne
248 very quality] vtmost pleasure
257 Let ... voice] Your voyces Lords: beseech you let
     her will] Have a free way
266 Of ... seel] And ... foyles
267 officed] actiue
271 estimation] reputation

280 import] concerne
289 if thou hast eyes] haue a quicke eye
347 Therefore] shee must haue change, she must.
     Therefore
362 conjunctive] communicatiue
387 plume] make

II.1

  8 mountains melt on them] the huge mountaine meslt
 12 chidden] chiding
 15 ever-fixèd] euer fired
 20 lads] Lords
 68 high] by
 72 mortal] common
 80 Make . . . in] And swiftly come to
 95 See for the news] So speakes this voyce
167 gyve] catch
179 calms] calmenesse
235 slipper and subtle] subtle slippery
286 lusty] lustfull

II.3

 51 else] lads
129 Prizes the virtue] Praises the vertues
143 twiggen-bottle] wicker bottle
187 mouths] men
200 collied] coold
313 broken joint] braule
357-8 and so . . . Venice] as that comes to, and no money
     at all, and with that wit returne to Venice

III.1

 41 sure] soone

III.2

  2 senate] State

III.3

 70 mammering] muttering
114 conceit] counsell
122 dilations] denotements
124 be sworn] presume
153 What dost thou mean] Zouns
352 rude] wide

353 dread clamours] great clamor
358 mine] mans
373 lov'st] liuest
463 execution] excellency

III.4

51 sorry] sullen
62 loathèd] lothely
145 observancy] obseruances
174 continuate] conuenient

IV.1

80 return] retire
82 fleers] Ieeres
213 I . . . Lodovico] Something from Venice sure, tis
       Lodouico

IV.2

17 their wives] her sex
46 I have lost] Why I haue left
47 they rained] he ram'd
169 The . . . meat] And the great Messengers of Venice
       stay
190 acquaintance] acquittance
207 exception] conception
232 harlotry] harlot

IV.3

103 uses] vsage

V.1

7 stand] sword
8 deed] dead
11 quat] gnat
14 gain] game
34 unblest fate hies] fate hies space
76–7 my sweet Cassio,] O Cassio, Cassio, Cassio]
       O my sweete Cassio!] Cassio, Cassio
86 be . . . injury] beare a part in this
105 gentlemen] Gentlewoman
106 gastness] ieastures

V.2

10 thy light] thine
13 relume] returne

15 needs must] must needes
55 conception] conceit
70 hath used thee] hath – vds death
111 nearer] neere the
149 iterance] iteration
208 reprobance] reprobation
217 'Twill ... peace?] 'Twill out, 'twill, I hold my peace sir, no.
218 I will speak as ... north] Ile be in speaking ... ayre
285 Wrench] wring
347 med'cinable] medicinal
359 loading] lodging

5 Emendations

I.1

30 leed] be-leed F; led Q
152 stand] stands Q, F
155 hell pains] hell apines F; hells paines Q

I.2

11 For be assured] Be assur'd F; For be sure Q
50 carack] Carract F; Carrick Q

I.3

58 yet] it Q, F
87 feats of broil] Feats of Broiles F; feate of broyle Q
177 company] noble company Q, F
217 piecèd] pierced Q, F
228 couch] Cooch Q; Coach F
232 war] Warres Q, F
261 In me] In my Q, F
323 beam] ballance Q; braine F
336 thou these] thou the F; these Q

II.1

13 mane] Maine Q, F
65 tire the ingener] tyre the Ingeniuer F; beare all excellency Q
67 He's] He has Q; Ha's F
70 enscarped] ensteep'd F; enscerped Q
108 of doors] of doore F; adores Q

195 let's] let vs Q, F
294 I leash] I trace F; I crush Q

II.2

5 addiction] addition F; minde Q

II.3

112 well] well then Q, F
121 in him] him in Q, F
161 sense of place] place of sense Q, F
212 leagued] league Q, F
221 following] following him Q, F
260 of sense] sence F; offence Q
308 denotement] deuotement Q, F

III.1

25 General's wife] Ceneral's wife Q; General F

III.2

6 We'll] Well F; We Q

III.3

119 affright me more] fright me the more F; affright me
     the more Q
147 that ... then] that your wisedome F; I intreate you
     then Q
168 fondly] soundly F; strongly Q
180 exsufflicate] exufflicate Q, F
182 fair, loves] faire, feeds well, loues Q, F
202 keep't] kept F; keepe Q
209 to] too Q, F
347 make] makes Q, F
403 circumstance] circumstances Q, F
437 any that] any it Q, F
452 feels] keepes F

III.4

42 there's] heere's Q, F
82 an] and Q, F
112 sorrow] sorrowes Q, F
143 Our] our other Q, F

IV.1

73 shall] she shall Q, F
87 gestures] ieasture Q, F

101 construe] conster Q; conserue F

123 win] winnes Q, F

IV.2

63 Ay, there] I heere Q, F

79 hear it] hear't Q, F

167 It is so] It is but so F; Tis but so Q

175 daff'st] dafts F; doffts Q

IV.3

38 sighing] singing F

V.1

22 But ... hear] But so ... heard F; be't so ... hear Q

114 quite] quite dead F; dead Q

V.2

107 murder] Murthers Q, F

216 O God! O heavenly Powers] Oh Heauen! Oh
heauenly Powres F; O God, O heauenly God Q

233 serve] serues Q, F

288 wast] wert Q; was F

346 Drop] Drops Q, F

6 Stage Directions

I.1

82 *above*] F; *at a window* Q

145 *Exit above*] *Exit* F; *not in* Q

160 *in his night-gown*] *not in* F

I.2

33 *Enter ... torches*] *Enter Cassio, with Torches* F; *Enter
Cassio with lights, Officers and Torches* Q (*both at
line* 27)

49 *Exit*] *not in* Q, F

53 *Enter Othello*] *not in* Q, F

I.3

0 *The Duke ... attendants*] *Enter Duke, Senators, and
Officers* F; *Enter Duke, and Senators set at a Table,
with lights and Attendants* Q

121 *Exit ... attendants*] *Exit two or three* Q; *not in* F

291 *Exeunt ... attendants*] *Exit* F; *Exeunt* Q

297 *Exeunt ... Desdemona] Exit Moore and Desdemona*
Q; *Exit* F

II.1

55 *Salvo]* not in F; *A shot* Q
82 *and attendants]* not in Q, F
99 *He kisses Emilia]* not in Q, F
121 *(aside)]* not in Q, F
164 *(aside)]* not in Q, F
173 *Trumpet] Trumpets within* Q; not in F
174 *(aloud)]* not in Q, F
191 *They kiss]* not in F
206 *Exeunt ... Roderigo] Exit* Q; *Exit Othello and*
Desdemona F

II.3

11 *and attendants]* not in Q, F
59 *and servants with wine]* not in Q, F
132 *Exit Roderigo]* not in F
139 *(Cry within)]* not in F
145 *He strikes Roderigo]* not in Q, F
154 *Bell rings]* not in Q, F
247 *Montano is led off] Lead him off* Q, F
251 *Exeunt ... Cassio] Exit Moore, Desdemona, and*
attendants Q; *Exit* F

III.3

239 *(going)]* not in Q, F
284 *He ... it]* not in Q, F
312 *(snatching it)]* not in Q, F

III.4

34 *(Aside)]* not in Q, F

IV.1

43 *He falls] Falls in a Traunce* F; *he fals downe* Q
58 *Exit Cassio]* not in Q, F
92 *Othello retires]* not in Q, F
109, 112, 114 etc. *(aside)]* not in Q, F
168 *Exit Cassio]* not in F
169 *(coming forward)]* not in Q, F
212 *Trumpet sounds]* not in Q, F
216 *He ... letter]* not in Q, F
217 *He ... letter]* not in Q, F

240 *He strikes her*] *not in* Q, F
262 *Exit Desdemona*] *not in* Q, F

IV.2

89 *(Calling)*] *not in* Q, F

IV.3

9 *Othello . . . attendants*] *not in* Q, F
38 etc. *(sings)*] *not in* Q, F
44 etc. *(She speaks)*] *not in* Q, F

V.I

7 *He retires*] *not in* Q, F
26 *He wounds Roderigo*] *not in* Q, F
     Iago . . . exit] *not in* Q, F
27 *above*] *not in* Q, F
46 *with a light*] *not in* F
61 *He stabs Roderigo*] *not in* Q, F
62 *He faints*] *not in* Q, F
64 *Lodovico . . . forward*] *not in* Q, F
98 *Enter . . . chair*] *not in* Q, F
104 *Cassio . . . removed*] *not in* Q, F
110 *Enter Emilia*] *not in* F
128 *(Aside)*] *not in* Q, F

V.2

0 *with a light*] *not in* F
   Desdemona in her bed] *not in* Q
15 *He kisses her*] *not in* F
85 *smothers*] Q; *stifles* F
106 *(He unlocks door)*] *not in* Q, F
120 *She . . . curtains*] *not in* Q, F
197 *(falling on bed)*] *Oth, fals on the bed* Q; *not in* F
199 *(rising)*] *not in* Q, F
233 *He . . . exit*] *not in* F; *The Moore runnes at Iago.*
     Iago kils his wife Q
249 *She dies*] *not in* F
269 *He goes to the bed*] *not in* Q, F
279 *in a chair*] *not in* F
352 *He stabs himself*] *not in* F
355 *falls on the bed and*] *not in* Q, F
361 *The . . . drawn*] *not in* Q, F

The Songs

For a full discussion see *Music in Shakespearean Tragedy* by F. W. Sternfeld (1963), from whose work the following notes are, with his permission, derived.

1. 'And let me the canakin clink' (II.3.64)
The tune for this song is not certainly known, but the following tune called 'A Soldier's Life' fits the words. It appears to be traditional, though not printed until 1651 (in John Playford's *The English Dancing Master*). A version of it is familiar as the tune to which, according to stage tradition, Ophelia sings 'Tomorrow is St Valentine's Day' in *Hamlet* (IV.5.46).

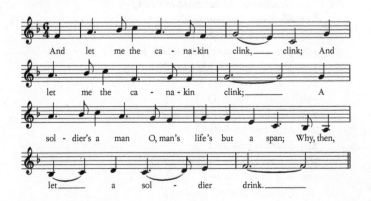

2. 'King Stephen was and-a worthy peer' (II.3.84)
A song with the refrain 'Then take thy auld cloak about thee' is
found in the eighteenth century and the music may be a version
of that used for this well-known ballad in Shakespeare's time.
The tune was first printed in James Oswald's *Caledonian Pocket
Companion* (mid eighteenth century); and the following vocal
version appeared in Robert Bremner's *Thirty Scots Songs for a
Voice and Harpsichord* (1757, as revised in 1770).

King Ste - phen was and-a wor - thy peer, His
bree - ches cost him but a crown; He held them six - pence
all too dear; With that he called the tai - lor lown. He
was a wight of high re-nown, And thou art but of
low de-gree; 'Tis pride that pulls the coun-try down; Then
take thine auld cloak a - bout thee.

3. 'The poor soul sat sighing by a sycamore tree' (IV.3.38)

This song was well known. Different settings appear in manuscripts of the sixteenth century and later. The following, which is the only one for voice and lute, seems to be the version most easily adjusted to the words in Shakespeare's text. It is found in a manuscript in the British Museum (Add MSS. 15117, folio 18) dated 1616 or earlier.

Commentary

Biblical references are to the Bishops' Bible (1568, etc.), the official English translation of Elizabeth's reign.

I.I

The play opens at night, in the street outside Brabantio's house in the middle of a conversation between Iago and Roderigo, described in the Folio (F) list of characters as *a Villaine* and *a gull'd Gentleman*. Although the opening scenes of Shakespeare's plays are expository, the facts are here distorted by Iago's envy and by his anxiety not to be deprived of Roderigo's money. Iago has been as surprised as his dupe by Desdemona's marriage.

4 *'Sblood*: God's blood. This and other oaths were omitted in F because of the new regulations against profanity. Iago's oaths contrast with Roderigo's feeble *Tush*.

8–33 *Despise me, if I do not ... his Moorship's Ancient*: We cannot assume that Iago's account is accurate or that the main cause of his hatred of Othello is Cassio's promotion. See Introduction, pp. xliii–xliv.

13 *bombast circumstance*: Bombastic beating about the bush.

14 *stuffed*: Bombast was originally cotton used for stuffing quilts and clothes.

16 *Non-suits*: Rejects the suit of.
Certes: Certainly.

19 *arithmetician*: Iago means that Cassio's knowledge of war was theoretical.

21 *A fellow almost damned in a fair wife*: Possibly at this
point in the play Shakespeare intended to give Cassio
a wife and afterwards decided to fuse the harlot and
the lady (*donna*) of the source. There were Italian and
English proverbs on the damnation involved in having
a fair wife – because she was certain to be seduced.

24 *theoric*: Theory.

25 *togèd*: Shakespeare is thinking of the Venetian government in terms of ancient Roman senators, wearing
togas. The F reading, *tongued*, accepted by few editors,
would mean that the senators could prattle about military matters without having any practical experience
of them.

30 *leed*: Cut off from the wind. This is clearly the intention of the Quarto (Q) *led*; the F reading *be be-leed* is
awkward to speak. Iago's matter-of-fact nautical
imagery contrasts with the imaginative sea-imagery of
Othello.

31 *counter-caster*: One who reckons with counters.

33 *Ancient*: Ensign.

36 *letter and affection*: Influence and nepotism. But Iago
had himself pulled strings (8).

37 *gradation*: Process of advancing step by step.

39 *affined*: Constrained.

44 *truly*: Faithfully.
shall mark: Cannot help noticing.

45 *knave*: Servant.

47 *ass*: Both Iago and Othello make frequent use of animal
imagery.

48 *cashiered*: He is cashiered. The elliptical expression is
characteristic of Iago.

49 *Whip me*: Ethical dative.

52 *shows*: Appearances.

53 *lined their coats*: Feathered their nests.

58 *Were I the Moor, I would not be Iago*: If I were the
General, I would not wish to be a subordinate.

61 *peculiar*: Personal.

63 *figure*: Shape, intention.

64 *compliment extern*: Outward show.

66 *I am not what I am*: This is thought by some to be a
parody of Exodus 3:14: 'I am that I am', and by others
to mean 'I am not what I seem to be'. Iago means
merely that, if he were to wear his heart on his sleeve,
he would cease to be himself.

67 *full*: Perfect.

thick-lips: This is the first indication that Othello is
negroid.

owe: Own.

68 *If he can carry't thus*: If he can get away with it.

her father: Desdemona's father, Brabantio.

73 *chances*: Possibilities.

76 *timorous*: Causing fear.

82 *at a window*: On the Elizabethan stage the window
would be at the side on the balcony level.

87 *Zounds*: God's wounds.

robbed . . . gown: A quibble may be intended on *robbed*
and 'robed'.

88 *burst*: Broken.

90 *tupping*: Covering.

91 *snorting*: Snoring.

92 *devil*: The devil was depicted as black.

100 *distempering*: Intoxicating.

101 *bravery*: Show of courage.

102 *start*: Startle.

103 *Sir, sir, sir*: Roderigo's words are extra-metrical, and
Brabantio continues without a pause.

107 *grange*: Country house.

108 *simple*: Sincere.

112 *Barbary*: The Barbary coast, North Africa, famous for
horse-breeding. Iago is, of course, referring to the
Moor.

114 *jennet*: Small Spanish horse.

germans: Near relations.

117–18 *making the beast with two backs*: Engaging in sexual
intercourse. In fact, as we learn later, Othello's marriage
is consummated in Act II.

119 *You are a Senator*: Many editors assume that Iago
suppresses an uncomplimentary word, but he may

either be ironically polite or pretending that *Senator* is
uncomplimentary.

123 *partly*: In some degree (from your apparent lack of
concern).

124 *odd-even*: Between midnight and 1 a.m.

126 *knave*: Servant.

127 *Moor —*: Roderigo does not complete his sentence.

128 *allowance*: Permission.

132 *from the sense of all civility*: Contrary to good manners.

137 *extravagant and wheeling*: Vagrant.

143 *accident*: Event.

149 *check*: Reprimand.

150 *cast*: Dismiss.
    embarked: Engaged.

152 *stand in act*: Are in progress.

153 *fathom* ability: This is one of Iago's admissions about
the man he hates.

159 *Sagittary*: The name of the inn or the house where
Othello and Desdemona are lodging.

160 *night-gown*: Dressing-gown.

162 *despisèd time*: A father whose daughter married
without his permission would be regarded as dishon-
oured.

172 *charms*: Enchantments (the first of many references to
witchcraft).

173 *property*: Nature.

I.2

The calm dignity of Othello on his first appearance
contrasts with what Iago and Brabantio have said about
him in the previous scene.

1–10 *Though in the trade of war ... I did full hard forbear
him*: Iago is posing as a loyal follower of Othello, in
accordance with the hypocritical course of conduct
outlined in the first scene, and ascribing to Roderigo
his own descriptions of the Moor. He has apparently
told Othello that Roderigo was responsible for informing Brabantio of Desdemona's elopement.

2 *very stuff*: Essence (but carrying on the metaphor of
trade).

3 *contrived*: Accent on first syllable.

5 *yerked*: Thrust.

10 *full hard*: With great difficulty.

12 *Magnifico*: Brabantio's title.

13 *potential*: Powerful.

18 *signory*: Venetian government.

19 *yet to know*: Not yet known.

21 *provulgate*: Publish abroad. As this is a rarer word than *promulgate* (F), it is unlikely to have been a misprint.

22 *siege*: Rank.
   demerits: Deserts.

23 *unbonneted*: Without my hat on, with all due modesty.

26 *unhousèd*: Without a house.

27 *circumscription and confine*: Restriction and restraint.

28 *yond*: Yonder.

31 *parts*: Natural gifts.
   perfect soul: Clear conscience.

33 *Janus*: Two-faced Roman god – the oath is appropriate to the two-faced Iago.

39 *divine*: Guess.

40 *heat*: Urgency.

44 *hotly*: Urgently.

50 *carack*: Large ship.

52 *who*: Whom.

53 *Marry*: The Virgin Mary (with a quibble on the word).
   Have with you: I'll go with you.

58 *Come, sir, I am for you*: Iago pretends to fight Roderigo.

59 *Keep up your bright swords, for the dew will rust them*: This exhibits Othello's calm authority rather than his supposed tendency to self-dramatization.

63 *enchanted*: See note to I.1.172.

67 *opposite*: Opposed.

70 *guardage*: Guardianship.

72 *gross in sense*: Quite obvious.

74 *minerals*: One of many references to poison.

75 *motion*: Impulses, faculties.

77 *attach*: Arrest.

79 *arts inhibited*: The black art.
   out of warrant: Unwarrantable.

86 *direct session*: Immediate sitting of court.

95 *idle*: Trifling.

99 *Bondslaves and pagans shall our statesmen be*: An oblique allusion, perhaps, to the historical fact that the Turks conquered Cyprus in 1570 and were its rulers thereafter. See Introduction, pp. lvii–lx.

I.3

The early part of this scene serves to emphasize Othello's military reputation and, more importantly, to demonstrate the need for discrimination and the avoidance of credulousness in dealing with dangers seen or unseen; the second part, containing Othello's defence of his wooing, is an effective rebuttal of Iago's slanders and Brabantio's accusations of witchcraft, and it shows that Desdemona was half the wooer; the third part, after the departure of the senators, reveals Iago's plot to retain his hold over Roderigo and the birth of his scheme to make Othello jealous of Cassio. This is prepared for by the accounts of Cassio in the first scene and his brief and colourless appearance in the second.

1 *composition*: Consistency.

2 *disproportioned*: Inconsistent.

5 *jump*: Tally.

6–7 *where the aim reports | 'Tis oft with difference*: Where there are discrepancies between one report and another.

10 *I do not so secure me in the error*: I do not feel myself so secure from the discrepancy between the various reports as not to believe the thing common to all.

11 *approve*: Endorse.

18 *assay*: Test.
   pageant: Show.

19 *in false gaʒe*: Looking in the wrong direction.

20 *importancy*: Importance.

23 *with more facile question bear it*: Capture it more easily.

24 *brace*: Readiness.

26 *dressed in*: Equipped with.

30 *wage*: Risk.

35 *injointed*: United.

37 *re-stem*: Retrace.

50 *I did not see you*: The Duke has been absorbed in his papers.

57 *engluts*: Swallows up.

64 *Sans*: Without.

67–9 *the bloody book of law | You shall yourself read in the bitter letter | After your own sense*: You shall be judge in your own cause and sentence the guilty one to death.

69 *proper*: Own.

70 *Stood*: Were accused.

80 *head and front*: Height and breadth.

81 *Rude am I in my speech*: There is nothing in the splendid poetry put into Othello's mouth to support this modest admission; but he is given an exotic vocabulary and a style which distinguishes his speech from that of the other characters.

90 *round*: Plain.

92 *conjuration*: Incantation.

95 *motion*: Movement of the soul, impulse.

96 *herself*: Itself.

105 *conjured*: Induced by magic spells (the accent is on the second syllable).

107 *more wider*: Fuller.

108 *thin habits*: Tenuous arguments.
    likelihoods: Hypotheses.

109 *modern*: Ordinary.

113 *question*: Talk.

122–3 *as truly as to heaven | I do confess the vices of my blood*: Othello, as we are reminded often, is a Christian.

128 *Still*: Continually.

138 *portance*: Behaviour.
    travels: This reading is superior to that of F, since *Trauellers* would imply that Othello's story had been embroidered.

139–44 *Wherein of antres vast and deserts idle ... Do grow beneath their shoulders*: These details were derived from Pliny's *Natural History* and from Elizabethan narratives of travel.

139 *antres*: Caves.
    idle: Uninhabited, sterile.

141　*hint*: Occasion.

143　*Anthropophagi*: Man-eaters.

150　*pliant*: Favourable.

152　*dilate*: Relate in full.

153　*by parcels*: Piecemeal.

154　*intentively*: Attentively, continuously.

158　*sighs*: The F reading, *kisses*, is obviously impossible.

162　*her*: Desdemona wished she could have been a man to have had such adventures; she was not suggesting that she would like to have such a husband.

165　*hint*: Opportunity. Othello is not suggesting that Desdemona was fishing for a proposal, although the previous words seem to be a fairly direct hint.

171　*take up this mangled matter at the best*: Make the best of a bad job.

180　*education*: Upbringing.

181　*learn*: Teach.

186　*challenge*: Claim.

187　*bu'y*: Be with you.

189　*get*: Beget.

193　*For your sake*: On your own account.

195　*escape*: Elopement.

196　*clogs*: Blocks of wood fastened to legs.

198　*grise*: Step.

200–217　*When remedies are past . . . piecèd through the ear*: The rhymed verse suggests that both the Duke and Brabantio are indulging in proverbial wisdom, and the speeches have a choric effect.

207　*bootless*: Vain.

217　*piecèd*: Mended.
　　　through the ear: By listening to consolation.

218　*I humbly beseech you to proceed to th'affairs of state*: The drop into prose indicates the change of subject.

220　*fortitude*: Strength.

222　*allowed*: Acknowledged.
　　　opinion: Public opinion.

223　*more safer*: Safer.

224　*slubber*: Spoil.

225　*stubborn*: Inflexible.

227 *tyrant, custom*: Proverbial.

229 *agnize*: Acknowledge.

230–31 *A natural and prompt alacrity* | *I find in hardness*: I am eager to embrace hardship.

233 *bending to your state*: Bowing to your office.

234 *disposition*: Arrangements.

235 *Due reference of place*: Treatment as becomes her rank.
exhibition: Financial provision.

236 *besort*: Retinue.

237 *levels*: Fits.

242 *unfolding*: Proposal.
prosperous: Favourable.

243 *charter*: Pledge.

247–8 *My heart's subdued* | *Even to the very quality of my lord*: I am in love with Othello's virtues.

253 *moth*: Condemned to useless idleness.

254 *rites*: Of marriage. Desdemona's frankness about sex contrasts with her husband's later protestations that he is anxious merely for companionship; but several editors prefer 'rights' – her right to share Othello's life.

257 *Let her have your voice*: Some critics suppose that the senators here show astonishment that Othello should ask to take his wife on active service; but if this had been Shakespeare's intention he would have made the Duke express surprise.

260 *comply with*: Satisfy.
affects: Desires.

261 *In me defunct – and proper satisfaction*: The line is probably corrupt in both texts, but the general meaning is clear. Othello is explaining that he is no longer a young man swayed by passion, and that he wants Desdemona's companionship more than the gratification of his own *proper* desires. Those who think that Othello is deceived about himself fasten on this line.

263 *defend*: Forbid.

266 *seel*: Blind (from the practice of sewing up the eyelids of a hawk).

267 *speculative and officed instruments*: Eyes and other faculties.

268 *disports*: Sexual pleasures.

269 *skillet*: Small metal pot, used in cooking.

270 *indign*: Unworthy.

271 *estimation*: Reputation.

279 *quality and respect*: Importance and relevance.

280 *import*: Concern.

281 *A man he is of honesty and trust*: The audience is aware that Othello is completely deceived about Iago and has no idea that he bears resentment at being passed over.

286 *delighted*: Delightful.

287 *far more fair than black*: This contrast between black and white recurs frequently throughout the play.

289–90 *Look to her, Moor, if thou hast eyes to see. | She has deceived her father, and may thee*: Iago remembers this couplet (see III.3.204).

294 *in the best advantage*: At the best opportunity.

296 *direction*: Instructions.

298–398 *Iago ... the world's light*: On Shakespeare's unlocalized stage the scene ceases to be the council-chamber when Roderigo and Iago are left alone.

302 *incontinently*: Forthwith.

306 *prescription*: This is a quibble on medical prescription and 'immemorial right' (A. Walker).

312 *guinea-hen*: Prostitute.

320 *gender*: Kind.

322 *corrigible authority*: Corrective power.

323 *beam*: Balance.

327 *unbitted*: Unbridled.

328 *sect*: Cutting.

331–2 *It is merely a lust of the blood and a permission of the will*: This is Iago's real opinion, though he is using it to corrupt Roderigo. He has been paid by Roderigo to arrange a marriage with Desdemona; he now holds out the hope that she can be seduced.

334 *perdurable*: Long-lasting.

335 *stead*: Benefit.

337 *defeat thy favour*: Disguise your face.

    usurped: Wrongly appropriated (because Roderigo is unmanly) or false.

341 *sequestration*: Separation.
344 *locusts*: Cobs of the carob tree.
345 *acerbe*: Bitter (the reading of F).
     coloquintida: Colocynth (bitter apple used as purgative drug).
349 *Make*: Raise.
350 *erring*: Wandering, sinful.
361 *hearted*: Heart-felt.
362 *conjunctive*: Allied.
365 *Traverse*: About turn!
370 *betimes*: Early.
377–98 *Thus do I ever make my fool my purse ... the world's light*: In Iago's soliloquy we see him for the first time without a mask.
384 *holds me well*: Esteems me.
386 *proper*: Handsome.
387 *plume up*: Set a feather in the cap of.
391 *dispose*: Disposition.
393–4 *The Moor is of a free and open nature, | That thinks men honest that but seem to be so*: This is another tribute from the villain about the hero, though it is said with a sneer.
397–8 *Hell and night | Must bring this monstrous birth to the world's light*: Iago deliberately chooses evil.

II.1

The rest of the play is set in Cyprus. Enough time has elapsed to enable the chief characters to sail to the island from Venice. The scene is near the harbour. On the symbolic significance of the storm, see Introduction, p. lxiii.

 7 *ruffianed*: Raged.
 8 *mountains*: Mountainous seas.
10 *segregation*: Dispersal.
11 *banning*: Cursing. This reading is superior to the colourless 'foaming'.
13 *monstrous mane*: The seas are compared to a wild beast.
15 *guards of th'ever-fixèd Pole*: Two stars in the Little Bear known as the Guardians.
16 *molestation*: Disturbance.

17 *enchafèd*: Angry.

22 *designment*: Design.

23 *sufferance*: Damage.

26 *Veronesa*: Presumably this was a vessel fitted out by Verona, which belonged to Venice; but it has been suggested that the word should be *verrinessa*, or cutter. (Shakespeare, to judge from *The Two Gentlemen of Verona*, thought that town was a port.)

30 *'tis a worthy governor*: Another tribute to Othello.

32 *sadly*: Gravely.

39 *th'aerial blue*: The sky.

40 *An indistinct regard*: Indistinguishable.

41 *expectancy*: Expectation.

42 *more arrivance*: Arrival of more ships.

49 *allowance*: Reputation.

50–51 *not surfeited to death,* | *Stand in bold cure*: Are not excessive, but healthy.

55 *My hopes do shape him for*: I hope it is.

60 *is your General wived*: There has been no previous mention of Othello's marriage. Possibly some lines have dropped out, for Montano has had no private conversation with Cassio.

62 *paragons*: Equals or excels.

64–5 *And in th' essential vesture of creation* | *Does tire the ingener*: 'In real beauty or outward form goes beyond the power of the artist's inventive or expressive pencil' (Hudson). But *ingener* is an emendation of *Ingeniuer* and *tyre* can mean 'attire', as well as 'weary'. Possibly *tire* was suggested by *vesture* through an unconscious quibble.

69 *guttered*: With gullies, jagged.

70 *enscarped to clog*: Nearly all editors accept *ensteeped* from F but reject *enclogge*. It seems probable that *enscerped* was a misprint for *enscarped* (that is, shelved abruptly). This fits the rocks, if not the sands; and Shakespeare may have been responsible for both readings.

72 *mortal*: Deadly. Here again the alternative reading 'common' makes good sense.

76 *footing*: Landing.

77 *se'nnight*: Week.

80 *Make love's quick pants*: This weak phrase was substituted for an even feebler phrase in Q.

87 *Enwheel*: Encircle.

94 *greeting*: By firing a salvo.

99 *courtesy*: Kissing was a normal method of greeting, and does not imply that Cassio was flirting with Emilia.

107 *chides with thinking*: Does not utter her shrewish thoughts.

108 *pictures*: That is, silent.

109 *bells*: That is, noisy.

111 *housewives*: Hussies.

119 *assay*: Try.

121–2 *I am not merry, but I do beguile | The thing I am by seeming otherwise*: This is merely an explanation to the audience, so that Desdemona should not appear too little concerned for Othello's safety.

125 *as birdlime does from frieze*: Frieze or frize is a coarse cloth, and when one tries to remove birdlime from it one pulls out the threads at the same time. So Iago's powers of invention are 'sticky'.

130 *witty*: Clever.

black: Brunette.

132 *white*: With a quibble on 'wight'.

135 *folly*: Wantonness.

136 *fond*: Foolish.

138 *foul*: Ugly or sluttish.

144 *put on the vouch*: Compel the approval.

152 *change the cod's head for the salmon's tail*: This passage is obscure, probably obscene, in view of the connotations of cod's *head* and *tail*; but it may merely mean exchange a foolish husband for a handsome lover.

157 *small beer*: Trivial events.

160 *profane*: Worldly.

161 *liberal*: Licentious.

162 *home*: Bluntly.

162–3 *relish him more in*: Appreciate him more in the role of.

167 *gyve*: Fetter, ensnare.

167–8 *You say true, 'tis so indeed*: This is either a comment
on the animated conversation between Cassio and
Desdemona or a reply (not spoken aloud) to Cassio's
last remark (162–3).

171 *sir*: Gentleman.

173 *clyster-pipes*: Tubes used for injection (here used
obscenely).

176 *fair warrior*: Othello is referring to her courage in
accompanying him to the wars, and unconsciously
echoing the language of sonneteers. He may also be
thinking of her wish that she had been a man.

183–9 *If it were now to die ... Amen to that, sweet Powers*:
Dramatic irony.

194 *set down the pegs*: Slacken the strings.

198 *desired*: Liked.

200 *out of fashion*: Unbecomingly.

205 *challenge*: Claim.

207–8 *Do thou meet me presently at the harbour*: These lines
are spoken not to Roderigo, but to one of the soldiers
who are to fetch Othello's luggage.

207 *presently*: At once.

215 *thus*: On the lips.

223 *favour*: Appearance.

225 *conveniences*: Points of fitness.

229 *pregnant*: Cogent.

231 *conscionable*: Conscientious.

233 *humane*: Polite.
      salt: Lustful.

235 *slipper*: Slippery.
      occasions: Opportunities.

236 *stamp*: Coin.

243 *condition*: Characteristics.

244 *fig's end*: Worthless thing.

247 *paddle with*: Stroke.

254 *incorporate*: Bodily.

259 *tainting*: Sneering at.

261 *minister*: Provide.

263 *choler*: Anger.

266 *qualification*: Dilution, appeasement.

271 *prosperity*: Success.

277–303 *That Cassio loves her . . . never seen till used*: See Introduction, p. xlv.

280 *constant, loving, noble*: A notable testimonial from an enemy.

284 *accountant*: Accountable.

285 *diet*: Feed.

294 *leash*: Neither *crush* (Q) nor *trace* (F) makes good sense. The usual emendation 'trash' (check) is inappropriate to Roderigo, though it, like *quick hunting*, may be ironical. J. Dover Wilson adopts *leash* from an earlier conjecture.

295 *stand the putting on*: Do what I incite him to.

296 *on the hip*: At my mercy.

297 *rank garb*: Gross manner, as a cuckold.

II.2

This proclamation is a preparation for the drinking scene which follows, and also a reminder of Othello's strong sense of duty. See Introduction, p. xxviii.

3 *mere*: Absolute.

8 *offices*: For the supply of food and drink.

II.3

This scene is in the guardroom of the castle. The remaining scenes of the play are in or near the castle. Iago engineers the brawl between Roderigo and Cassio – Shakespeare deviates from his source in this respect – and persuades Cassio to appeal to Desdemona for reinstatement.

1, 7 *Michael*: Note the affectionate use of Cassio's Christian name.

7 *with your earliest*: At your earliest convenience.

9 *the fruits are to ensue*: The marriage has not been consummated.

13–25 *Not this hour . . . She is indeed perfection*: Iago's pruriency about Desdemona is contrasted with Cassio's chaste admiration.

14 *cast*: Dismissed.

21–2 *sounds a parley to provocation*: Arouses lustful thoughts.

27 *stoup*: Jug.

33–4 *I'll drink for you*: I'll drink in your place (that is, drink
more than my share, to cover your abstemiousness).

36 *qualified*: Mixed with water.

43 *dislikes*: Displeases.

50 *pottle-deep*: To the bottom of a two-quart tankard.

51 *swelling*: Lively.

52 *hold their honours in a wary distance*: Are quick to take
offence at any suspected insult.

53 *elements*: Quintessence.

58 *consequence*: What happens.
approve: Substantiate.

60 *rouse*: Large glass.

64–8 *And let me the canakin clink*: See The Songs, p. 154.

64 *canakin*: Small can.

67 *life's but a span*: Cf. Psalm 39:5: 'Behold thou hast made
my days as it were an hand breadth long.'

72 *potting*: Drinking.

77 *Almaine*: German.

84–91 *King Stephen . . . cloak about thee*: This song was earlier
than 1600; see The Songs, p. 155.

84 *and-a*: The syllable was inserted for the sake of the
tune.

87 *lown*: Loon, rogue.

96–9 *No, for I hold him to be unworthy . . . souls must not be
saved*: Cassio is already drunk, as Shakespeare indicates by his moralizing and theology.

104–5 *The Lieutenant is to be saved before the Ancient*: This is
likely to rub salt in Iago's wounds.

108 *my Ancient*: Another reference to Cassio's superior
rank.

125 *horologe*: Clock.
a double set: Twice round.

135 *ingraft*: Ingrafted.

143 *twiggen-bottle*: Bottle cased in wicker-work. This may
mean (1) beat Roderigo till he resembles wicker-work,
or (2) chase him through the holes in a wicker-work
case. The second explanation is more probable.

148 *mazzard*: Head.

155 *Diablo*: The Devil.

174 *quarter*: Friendship.

176 *unwitted*: Bereft of their wits. Believers in astrology thought that planets could drive men mad (cf. V.2.111–12).

179 *odds*: Quarrel.

185 *stillness*: Quietness, sobriety.

187 *censure*: Judgement.

189 *rich opinion*: High reputation.

193 *offends*: Hurts.

200 *collied*: Blackened.

204 *rout*: Brawl.

205 *approved*: Proved guilty.

210 *on the court and guard of safety*: In the guard-room, while actually members of the watch (who should protect the safety of the town).

212 *partially affined*: Bound by partiality.

leagued in office: Unwilling to testify against a superior.

214–40 *Touch me not so near . . . Which patience could not pass*: Iago has the difficult task of persuading both Othello and Cassio that he is minimizing the latter's fault, and of persuading Montano that he is not doing this.

245 *I'll make thee an example*: This seems to suggest that Othello is being severe because his wife has been disturbed.

247 *Montano is led off*: Both Q and F ascribe *Lead him off* to Othello, but it is probably a stage direction.

261–4 *Reputation is an idle and most false imposition . . . repute yourself such a loser*: Cf. III.3.154–60, where Iago says the opposite.

265 *cast*: Dismissed.

267–8 *beat his offenceless dog to affright an imperious lion*: Punish the innocent to deter the great criminal.

271 *slight*: Worthless.

272 *parrot*: Nonsense.

273 *fustian*: Bombast.

284 *applause*: Desire for applause.

295 *Hydra*: Snake with many heads slain by Hercules.

298 *ingredience*: Ingredients.

300 *familiar creature*: Friendly spirit.

310 *free*: Open.

314 *splinter*: Put a splint on.

328 *Probal*: Reasonable.

330 *subdue*: Persuade.

331 *fruitful*: Generous.

333 *renounce his baptism*: One of several references to Othello's faith.

337 *appetite*: Desire.

338 *function*: Exercise of faculties.

339 *parallel*: To Iago's plot.

340 *Divinity*: Theology.

341 *put on*: Incite.

354 *cry*: Pack.

365–6 *Though other things grow fair against the sun,* | *Yet fruits that blossom first will first be ripe*: The fact that you have already got Cassio dismissed means that you will soon enjoy Desdemona, despite the apparent happiness of her marriage.

375 *jump*: Exactly.

III.1

This scene follows soon after the conclusion of Act II, when day was already breaking. It was an Elizabethan custom to awaken a newly married couple with music. The Clown has little individuality and his jests are feeble. It has been argued that Shakespeare did not wish to lower the tension by arousing hearty laughter, but he need not have introduced a clown at all to act as a messenger.

1 *I will content your pains*: I will reward you for your trouble.

3–4 *have your instruments been in Naples*: An allusion to the results of the pox.

8–9 *tail . . . tale*: Indecent quibble.

19–20 *for I'll away*: Either a snatch of song or a misprint.

23 *quillets*: Quibbles.

30 *In happy time*: At the right moment.

39 *Florentine*: Cassio is surprised that Iago, a Venetian, should be as kind as one of his own fellow-countrymen.

48 *take the safest occasion by the front*: Seize on the first safe occasion.

54 *bosom*: Heart.

III.2

This little scene has two functions – to remind us of Othello's military responsibilities, and to prepare the way for his entrance with Iago in the next scene.

2 *do*: Convey.

3 *works*: Fortifications.

III.3

This is the longest scene in the play. At the beginning Othello is perfectly happy in his marriage; at the end he has decided to murder Desdemona and Cassio. Unless we realize the extent to which Shakespeare has telescoped the action, we shall be bound to think that Othello was absurdly prone to jealousy, instead of *not easily jealous* as he claims at the end of the play. Desdemona's promise to Cassio to get him reinstated is a sign of her innocence and inexperience; not because she has any reason to fear Othello's jealousy, but because in her natural warmth and generosity she does not realize that she is interfering in professional matters.

12 *strangeness*: Estrangement.

15 *nice*: Thin.

16 *breed itself so out of circumstance*: Be so long delayed.

17 *supplied*: Filled up.

19 *doubt*: Fear.

20 *give thee warrant of*: Guarantee.

22 *My lord shall never rest*: Desdemona, however charmingly, is proposing to nag Othello until she gets her way.

23 *watch him tame*: Prevent him from sleeping (as hawks were tamed).

24 *shrift*: Confessional.

27 *solicitor*: Advocate.

35 *I like not that*: Iago begins his temptation.

47 *present*: Immediate.

67 *check*: Reprimand.

70 *mammering*: Stammering, hesitating.

71 *came a-wooing with you*: This is the first we hear of
Cassio's part in Othello's wooing and it is difficult to
reconcile with the Moor's own account in I.3. There
are four possible explanations: (1) Desdemona supposed that Othello was wooing her before he realized
it himself; (2) Othello gave a slightly distorted account
of the events leading up to his declaration; (3)
Desdemona is referring to the period between the
declaration and the elopement, though she would
hardly dispraise him then; (4) Shakespeare wanted to
give a lead to Iago's words later in the scene (93–4)
and did not bother about the discrepancy.

74 *bring him in*: Get him reinstated.

79 *peculiar*: Personal.

82 *poise*: Weight.

90 *wretch*: Term of endearment.

91 *But I do*: If I do not.

91–2 *And when I love thee not, | Chaos is come again*: This
proves to be prophetic.

106 *monster*: Cf. 164.

114 *conceit*: Idea.

119 *stops*: Pauses.

121 *of custom*: Customary.

122 *close dilations*: Involuntary delays.

126 *none*: Not to be men.

139 *leets*: Days on which courts are held.

146 *of*: The emendation 'oft' for *of* would improve the
syntax but is not really necessary.
jealousy: Suspicious nature.

148 *conjects*: Conjectures.

150 *scattering*: Random.

154–5 *Good name in man and woman, dear my lord, | Is the
immediate jewel of their souls*: Proverbial.

155 *immediate*: Nearest the heart.

167–8 *But O, what damnèd minutes tells he o'er, | Who dotes
yet doubts, suspects yet fondly loves*: This proves to be
Othello's fate.

169 *O misery*: Othello is not referring to himself.

170 *Poor and content is rich, and rich enough*: Proverbial.

171 *fineless*: Boundless.

176–7 *To follow still the changes of the moon | With fresh suspicions*: Indulge in new suspicions several times a month.

177–8 *No, to be once in doubt | Is once to be resolved*: If I once doubt, I will settle the question one way or the other (cf. 188–90).

178 *goat*: Supposed to be lustful.

180 *exsufflicate and blown*: Inflated and blown up (but some think the words mean 'spat out and fly-blown').

186 *doubt*: Suspicion.

198 *self-bounty*: Inherent generosity.

200–202 *In Venice they do let God see the pranks ... but keep't unknown*: Othello begins to be worried at this point because of his comparative ignorance of Venetian society.

204 *She did deceive her father, marrying you*: Echoing Brabantio's last words in I.3.

208 *seel*: Blind.
    oak: The grain of oak.

211 *I am bound to thee for ever*: With a possible quibble on *bound*.

217 *issues*: Conclusions.

220 *success*: Result.

223 *honest*: Chaste.

227 *affect*: Like.

230–31 *Foh! One may smell in such a will most rank, | Foul disproportion, thoughts unnatural*: This mention of difference of colour is Iago's strongest card. His earlier exclamation *Pish!* (II.1.255) and *Foh!* here suggest there is a streak of puritanism in him.

232 *in position*: Positively.

235 *fall to match*: Happen to compare.
    country: Country's.

236 *happily*: Maybe.

247 *means*: To recover his post.

248 *entertainment*: Reinstatement.

251 *busy*: Interfering.

253 *free*: Innocent.

254 *government*: Self-control.

257 *haggard*: Wild (a term in falconry).

258 *jesses*: Straps tied to legs of hawks.

260 *prey at fortune*: Fend for herself. At this point Othello is not thinking of killing Desdemona but only of casting her off.

    Haply: Perhaps.

261 *soft parts*: Pleasant arts.

262 *chamberers*: Gallants.

267 *toad*: Othello begins to use the characteristic animal imagery of Iago.

271 *Prerogatived*: Privileged.

273 *forkèd plague*: Cuckold's horns.

274 *do quicken*: Are conceived.

276 *I'll not believe't*: As soon as he sees Desdemona, Othello repudiates Iago's temptation; but the recovery of faith is only temporary.

277 *generous*: Noble.

282 *watching*: Not getting enough sleep.

284 *napkin*: Handkerchief. The loss of the handkerchief is Shakespeare's invention. In Cinthio's tale it is stolen. Desdemona forgets the precious love-token because, in her love for Othello, she is concerned about his 'headache'.

293 *ta'en out*: Copied.

296 *fantasy*: Whim.

299 *A thing*: Vagina.

313 *import*: Importance.

316 *Be not acknown on't*: Don't acknowledge anything about it.

323 *conceits*: Ideas.

324 *distaste*: Be distasteful.

325 *act*: Action.

327 *poppy*: Opium (derived from the poppy).

    mandragora: Narcotic plant.

328 *drowsy*: Causing sleep.

330 *owed'st*: Didst own.

337 *free*: Untroubled.

339–40 *He that is robbed, not wanting what is stolen, | Let him not know't, and he's not robbed at all*: Proverbial.

339 *wanting*: Missing.

343 *Pioners*: Sappers.

344 *So*: If.

351 *circumstance*: Pageantry.

352 *mortal*: Deadly.

353 *Jove's dread clamours*: Thunder.

362 *probation*: Proof.

372 *bu'y*: Be with.

373 *make thine honesty a vice*: By carrying it to excess.

376–7 *I thank you ... such offence*: The couplet underlines the fact that he is about to exit.

377 *sith*: Since.

379 *should*: Ought to be (quibbling on *shouldst* in the previous line).

381 *honest*: Chaste.

382 *just*: True.

384 *Dian*: Diana (goddess of chastity).

385–7 *If there be cords or knives, | Poison or fire or suffocating streams, | I'll not endure it*: Othello is thinking of suicide.

392 *supervisor*: Looker-on.

396 *bolster*: Share a bolster.

400 *prime*: Lecherous.

401 *salt*: Lustful.
     pride: Heat.

403 *imputation and strong circumstance*: Strong circumstantial evidence.

425 *foregone conclusion*: Previous consummation.

426 *shrewd doubt*: Cursed suspicion. This line is given to Othello in F, perhaps rightly.

429 *yet we see nothing done*: Referring to Othello's demand for ocular proof.

431 *Have you not sometimes seen a handkerchief*: Iago reserves this 'proof' till Othello is too upset to think clearly.

445 *hearted*: Seated in the heart.

446 *fraught*: Burden.

447 *aspics'*: Venomous snakes'.

450 *Pontic sea*: Black Sea.

453 *Propontic*: Sea of Marmora.
　　Hellespont: Dardanelles.
456 *capable*: Ample.
461 *clip*: Encompass.
463 *execution*: Activities.
　　wit: Intelligence.
465 *remorse*: Compassion. Iago means that the utmost
　　cruelty will be reckoned as kindness because he is
　　doing it for Othello.
466 *ever*: Soever.
476 *I am your own*: (1) I am your faithful servant; (2) you
　　have become possessed with my spirit.

III.4

24 *I know not*: Emilia's lie makes it difficult for her to
　　explain matters after Othello has shown his jealousy.
26 *crusadoes*: Gold coins.
31 *humours*: Bodily fluids determining temperament.
38 *fruitfulness*: Generosity or amorousness.
　　liberal: Generous or licentious.
40 *sequester*: Sequestration, removal.
47 *our new heraldry*: Possibly this is a topical reference.
　　The meaning is that people used 'to give their hands
　　and their hearts together, but we think it a finer grace
　　to look asquint, our hand looking one way, and our
　　heart another' (Sir William Cornwallis, 1601).
49 *chuck*: Term of endearment.
51 *salt and sorry rheum*: Wretched running cold.
57 *charmer*: Enchantress.
59 *amiable*: Beloved.
63 *fancies*: Loves.
69–72 *there's magic in the web of it ... prophetic fury sewed the
　　work*: The lines derive from Ariosto, *Orlando Furioso*
　　(1532), XLVI.80.
72 *prophetic fury*: '*Il furor profetico*' (Ariosto).
74 *mummy*: Preparation made from mummies.
79 *rash*: Rashly.
90 *talk*: Talk to.
101 *hungerly*: Hungrily.
104 *happiness*: Good luck.

109 *office*: Loyal service.

117 *shut myself up*: Confine myself.

121 *favour*: Appearance.

124 *blank*: Centre of target, range.

137 *unhatched practice*: Undisclosed plot.

139 *puddled*: Made muddy.

141–4 *'Tis even so . . . that sense | Of pain*: See An Account of the Text. Neither Q nor F gives a satisfactory text, but the sense is clear.

146 *bridal*: Wedding.

147 *unhandsome*: Inadequate.

warrior: Desdemona is thinking of Othello's greeting on his arrival in Cyprus (II.1.176).

151–3 *Pray heaven it be state matters . . . Concerning you*: Emilia is feeling guilty about the handkerchief.

152 *toy*: fancy.

157 *monster*: Cf. III.3.164.

169 *week*: Cassio, according to one time-scheme, arrived in Cyprus only on the previous day; but a week could elapse between III.3 and III.4. This, however, would conflict with Othello's demand at the end of III.3 that Cassio should be killed within three days and with the natural assumption that Othello would demand the handkerchief at the first opportunity.

174 *continuate*: Uninterrupted.

176 *Take me this work out*: Copy this embroidery for me.

197 *circumstanced*: Give way to circumstance.

IV.1

The opening of this scene indicates that despite Othello's determination to kill Desdemona he still loves her; and Iago, knowing that every hour she lives increases his own exposure, is driven to arouse Othello's rage by harping on the sexual relations of Cassio and Desdemona.

9 *So*: If.

21 *As doth the raven o'er the infected house*: A croaking raven was thought to portend death to the plague-stricken inmates of a house.

25 *abroad*: In the world.

27 *voluntary dotage*: Willing infatuation.

28 *Convincèd or supplied*: Overcome or gratified sexually.

38–9 *First to be hanged and then to confess*: This impossibility indicates Othello's hopeless· confusion of mind.

40 *shadowing*: Foreshadowing, darkening.

40–41 *without some instruction*: If there were no basis of fact.

41 *shakes*: Shake.

42 *Noses, ears, and lips*: Othello is thinking of the supposed love-making between Cassio and Desdemona.

50–51 *epilepsy.* | *This is his second fit*: Possibly an invention.

53 *lethargy*: Unconsciousness.

58 *on great occasion*: On an important matter.

60 *mock*: Othello thinks Iago is referring to the cuckold's horns.

64 *civil*: Civilized.

67 *May draw with you*: As though they were horned cattle.

68 *unproper*: Shared with a lover.

69 *peculiar*: Their own alone.

71 *lip*: Kiss.
   secure: Free from suspicion.

73 *what I am*: That is, a cuckold.
   what shall be: What will be my action (see An Account of the Text).

75 *a patient list*: Bounds of patience.

79 *ecstasy*: Fit.

81 *encave*: Hide.

82 *fleers*: Sneers.

86 *cope*: Meet (with a sexual undertone).

88 *all in all in spleen*: Quite transformed by passion.

92 *keep time*: Be restrained.

94 *housewife*: Hussy (pronounced 'huzif').

101 *unbookish*: Ignorant.

104 *addition*: Title.

108 *caitiff*: Wretch.

119 *Roman*: Referring to Roman triumphs.

120 *customer*: Harlot.

127 *scored*: Branded.

134 *sea-bank*: Sea-shore.

135 *bauble*: Plaything.

142–3 *but not that dog I shall throw it to*: When he has cut it off.

146 *such another*: This does not imply that Cassio fails to recognize Bianca; it is merely an idiomatic way of referring to a person one knows only too well. Pandarus, commenting on Cressida's bawdy talk in *Troilus and Cressida*, says 'You are such another!' (I.2. 257).

fitchew: Polecat, strumpet.

Enter Bianca: The arrival of Bianca with the handkerchief is a stroke of luck which Iago turns to good account.

154 *hobby-horse*: Harlot.

169–211 *How shall I murder him, Iago? ... You shall hear more by midnight*: This dialogue brings out the conflict between love and jealousy in Othello's mind, 'the struggle not to love her' (Coleridge).

199 *messes*: Pieces of meat.

204 *unprovide*: Make reluctant.

210 *be his undertaker*: Deal with him.

238 *on't*: Of it.

239 *I am glad to see you mad*: To rejoice at your lover's promotion. But possibly *mad* is an abbreviation of 'madam' and Desdemona is astonished at Othello's cold politeness.

245 *teem*: Be impregnated.

246 *falls*: Let fall.

252–6 *What would you with her ... And turn again*: Othello is pretending that Desdemona is a harlot and Lodovico a potential client.

259 *passion*: Grief.

265 *Goats and monkeys*: Cf. III.3.400.

269 *accident*: Fate.

272 *censure*: Judgement.

276 *use*: Custom.

IV.2

In this scene Othello treats his wife as though she were a prostitute and Emilia as a bawd; but though he accuses Desdemona of adultery, he does not give her a chance of defending herself by naming her supposed lover, her accuser or detailing the evidence against her.

20   *whore*: Desdemona.

21   *closet lock and key*: Concealer.

26   *Some of your function*: Do your office.

27   *procreants*: Those engaged in procreation.

29   *mystery*: Trade (of procuress).

42   *motive*: Cause.

46–7 *heaven ... they*: Shakespeare possibly wrote *God ... he*. See An Account of the Text.

53–4 *A fixèd figure for the time of scorn | To point his slow unmoving finger at*: Othello thinks of himself as an object of mockery, pointed at by the scornful time, as the figure on a clock or dial is pointed at by the hand, which moves so slowly that it seems not to move at all.

56   *garnered*: Stored.

61   *gender*: Engender.
     Turn thy complexion: Change colour.

64   *honest*: Chaste.

65   *shambles*: Butchers' slaughter-house.

66   *quicken*: Receive life.

72   *commoner*: Whore.

76   *moon*: Symbolizing chastity.
     winks: Shuts her eyes.

82   *vessel*: Body. Cf. 1 Thessalonians 4:3–4: 'that ye should abstain from fornication: That every one of you should know how to possess his vessel in holiness and honour.'

83   *other*: Of another man.

87   *I cry you mercy*: I beg your pardon.

103 *water*: Tears.

107–8 *stick | The smallest opinion on my least misuse*: Have the least suspicion of my least misbehaviour (Q reads *greatest abuse*: perhaps Shakespeare wrote *worst misuse*).

113 *I am a child to chiding*: I have had little experience of chiding.

120 *callet*: Drab.

128 *trick*: Whim, delusion.

131 *cogging*: Deceiving.
    to get some office: But Emilia does not suspect Iago.

137 *form*: Appearance.

140 *companions*: Fellows.

143 *within door*: Less loudly.

144 *squire*: Fellow.

146 *suspect me with the Moor*: Cf. II.1.286.

147 *go to*: An expression with a variety of meanings, here 'be quiet'.

152 *discourse*: Course.

154 *Delighted them*: Took delight.

155 *yet*: Still.

159 *defeat*: Destroy.

162 *addition*: Title.

170 *Enter Roderigo*: On Shakespeare's unlocalized stage it would not seem that Roderigo had sought out Iago in a private room of the castle.

175 *daff'st*: Dost put me off.

177 *conveniency*: Opportunity.

188 *votarist*: Nun, vowed to chastity

189 *sudden respect*: Immediate notice.

191–2 *go to*: See note to IV.2.147. Iago's use of the expression is probably accompanied by an obscene gesture. Roderigo means he cannot have sexual intercourse with Desdemona.

194 *fopped*: Duped.

203 *intendment*: Intention.

216 *engines for*: Plots against.

225 *determinate*: Conclusive.

232 *harlotry*: Harlot.

240 *high*: Fully.

IV.3

Now the time of Desdemona's murder approaches Othello has recovered his self-control. The song is omitted from the Q text probably because the boy who

played Desdemona could no longer sing. But some
critics think the song was added later.

11 *incontinent*: Forthwith.

19 *checks*: Rebukes.

22 *All's one*: All right.

26 *mad*: Faithless.

30–31 *I have much to do | But*: I find it difficult not.

33 *night-gown*: Dressing-gown.

34 *proper*: Handsome.

38–54 *The poor soul sat sighing . . . you'll couch with moe men*:
Adapted from an old song in which the forsaken lover
is a man. See The Songs, p. 156.

38 *sycamore*: Fig mulberry (not the modern sycamore).

39 *willow*: An emblem of forsaken love.

45 *these*: Necklace, jewels or other ornaments.

54 *moe*: More.

58–104 *Dost thou in conscience think . . . but by bad mend*: This
dialogue brings out the difference between Desde-
mona's innocence and idealism and Emilia's worldly-
wise cynicism and realism.

62 *heavenly light*: Moon.

67–8 *it is a great price for a small vice*: The rhyme suggests
that it is meant to be a quotation.

71–2 *joint ring*: Ring made in two separate parts

73 *exhibition*: Gift, allowance.

74 *Ud's*: God's.

83 *to th'vantage*: In addition.

84 *store*: Populate.

85 *But I do think it is their husbands' faults*: Emilia, who
has been speaking in prose, now drops into verse, to
give her words a kind of choric tone.

86 *duties*: Emilia is probably referring to sexual duties and
to Iago.

87 *foreign*: Other than their wives'.

88 *peevish jealousies*: Could refer to Iago or Othello.

90 *having*: Allowance.

   in despite: Out of spite.

91 *galls*: Spirits to resent.

103 *uses*: Habits.

104 *Not to pick bad from bad, but by bad mend*: Not to get worse through evil chance or suffering but to learn from it.

V.1

Iago, characteristically, gets Roderigo to attack Cassio, though he has to intervene himself; but he fails to kill either Cassio or Roderigo. Even without Emilia's evidence he would be ruined.

1 *bulk*: Projecting part of building. On the Elizabethan stage Roderigo would hide behind the pillar supporting the canopy.

2 *bare*: Unsheathed.

5 *resolution*: Pronounced with five syllables.

10 *'Tis but a man gone*: Roderigo is quoting Iago.
Forth my sword! He dies: He is rehearsing the murder in his mind.

11 *I have rubbed this young quat almost to the sense*: I have rubbed this pimple almost to the quick.

16 *bobbed*: Swindled.

19–20 *He hath a daily beauty in his life | That makes me ugly*: This might refer to Cassio's good looks, but more likely to his good manners and charm.

25 *coat*: Coat of mail, or leather jerkin.

27 *above*: On the balcony.

29 *It is even so*: Othello either mistakes Roderigo's voice for Cassio's and agrees that he is a villain, or else he continues his previous speech.

34–6 *And your unblest fate hies . . . with lust's blood be spotted*: Neither F nor Q is satisfactory and some critics think the lines were interpolated. It is odd that Othello should speak of *lust's blood* when he has decided to strangle or smother Desdemona.

36 *Enter Lodovico and Gratiano*: Gratiano has just arrived with news of Brabantio's death.

37 *passage*: Passers-by.

42 *heavy*: Gloomy, dark.

44 *come in to*: Approach.

69 *I cry you mercy*: Pardon me.

98 *that's well said*: Well done!

101 *Save you your labour*: Bianca is tending Cassio.

106 *gastness*: Frightened look.

122–3 *of life as honest | As you that thus abuse me*: Bianca is perhaps more honest, in one sense of the word, than Emilia.

129 *fordoes*: Undoes.

V.2

The bed was probably pushed forward from the curtained space under the balcony, as otherwise much of the action would be invisible to part of the audience It has often been observed that Othello has recovered something of his nobility at the beginning of this scene, but in his 'darkened reason' he believes he is sacrificing his wife to an ideal rather than committing a brutal murder. The actual deed, however, is committed not calmly but in a blind fury when Desdemona weeps for Cassio.

1 *cause*: Adultery.

4 *whiter skin of hers than snow*: Her skin whiter than snow.

7 *light . . . light*: (1) The torch; (2) Desdemona's life.

8 *flaming minister*: Serviceable torch. Cf. Psalm 104:4: 'He maketh his angels spirits: and his ministers a flaming fire.'

12 *Promethean*: Prometheus brought fire to men.

13 *relume*: Relight.

22 *It strikes where it doth love*: Cf. Hebrews 12:6: 'For whom the Lord loveth, he chasteneth.'

38 *When your eyes roll so*: This description was probably necessary on the Jacobean stage, where there was no artificial lighting. Cf. 43 below.

40 *They are loves I bear to you*: In deceiving her father.

47 *will – so*: There is a pause between these two words while Desdemona controls herself.

52 *presently*: At once.

55 *conception*: Belief.

59 *Offend*: Wrong.

63 *stone*: Turn to stone.

73 *ta'en order*: Taken steps.

83 *Being done, there is no pause*: Now the deed is begun, I cannot stop.

85 *O Lord, Lord, Lord*: Desdemona tries to pray; and Emilia's words in the next line seem like a macabre echo.

90 *So, so*: As suffocated persons do not recover consciousness, some actors and critics make Othello stab Desdemona. But Shakespeare may have been ignorant or, as some medical authorities suggest, Desdemona may die of shock.

94 *high*: Loud.

99 *O, insupportable! O heavy hour*: Othello already repents.

102 *yawn*: With an earthquake.
alteration: The change brought about by Desdemona's death.

105 *curtains*: Of the bed, to hide the body.

110 *error*: Straying off course.

125 *I myself*: Desdemona's lie, oddly condemned by some critics, is a final proof of her loving heart.

130 *She's like a liar gone to burning hell*: It has been suggested that Othello's violent repudiation of the lie indicates that he subconsciously realizes that if she had been unfaithful she would not have lied to save him.

131 *O, the more angel she*: Emilia's love for Desdemona leads her to risk her life, and finally to lose it. She is credibly transformed from the cynical spokesman of worldly wisdom at the end of the previous scene.

144 *chrysolite*: Semi-precious stone.

149 *iterance*: Repetition.

150 *made mocks with love*: Used love as a plaything (referring either to Desdemona's love for Othello or to her friendly intervention on behalf of Cassio).

182 *charm your tongue*: Be silent.

191 *I thought so then*: A reference either to IV.2.129 or to her misgiving when Iago takes the handkerchief.

206 *turn*: Deed.

208 *reprobance*: State of damnation.

211 *A thousand times*: This, obviously, could not have

happened during the course of the play, even when
every allowance has been made for 'double time'; but
Othello may be vaguely referring to the period before
and after his marriage.

212 *gratify*: Reward.

213 *recognizance*: Token.

216 *My father gave my mother*: But earlier (III.4.55–6)
Othello has told Desdemona that the handkerchief was
given to his mother by an Egyptian. The discrepancy
is probably an oversight, and could be resolved by the
assumption that Othello's father purchased the handkerchief from the Egyptian. But some critics implau-
sibly suggest that the earlier account was invented by
Othello to frighten Desdemona.

218 *liberal*: Unrestrainedly.
north: North wind.

231 *coxcomb*: Fool.

232–3 *Are there no stones in heaven | But what serve for the
thunder*: To punish such wickedness.

237 *notorious*: Notable.

242 *whipster*: One who whips out his sword (though
Montano, an experienced soldier, hardly deserves the
description).

243 *why should honour outlive honesty*: Why should reputation outlive desert?

251 *ice-brook's*: The sword was tempered by plunging it
into icy water. (It has been argued that *Isebrookes* – the
reading of Q – is a spelling of Innsbruck's; but the
definite article makes this impossible.)

256 *naked*: Unarmed.

262 *stop*: Power to stop me.

265 *butt*: Goal.

266 *sea-mark*: Beacon.

268 *Man*: Wield.

271 *compt*: Judgement day.

272–3 *This look of thine will hurl my soul from heaven | And
fiends will snatch at it*: Othello recognizes that he is
damned.

275 *slave*: Othello is speaking of himself, not of Iago.

283 *fable*: That a devil has cloven feet.

289 *practice*: Plot.
    slave: Villain.

291 *An honourable murderer, if you will*: See Introduction,
    pp. xxxvii–xxxix.

294 *consent*: Agree.

296 *Dear*: The epithet shows Cassio's noble forgiveness as
    well as his love for Othello.

310 *discontented*: Full of discontent.

313 *in the nick*: Of time.

317 *confessed*: Iago is willing to confess his deeds, but not
    his motives.

323 *cast*: Dismissed.

330 *hold him long*: Keep him long alive.

334 *Soft you*: One moment.

337 *unlucky*: Unfortunate.

342 *Perplexed*: Bewildered.

343 *Indian*: There are many stories of Indians throwing
    away precious stones: but the F reading, *Iudean*, also
    makes good sense if it is taken to refer to Judas. Cf.
    355.

344 *sùbdued eyes*: Overcome by grief, weeping.

347 *med'cinable gum*: Myrrh ('associated with incense, and
    therefore atonement and sacrifice' – A. Walker).

353 *period*: Ending.

357 *Spartan dog*: Notorious for their fierceness.

358 *fell*: Deadly.

362 *seize upon*: Take legal possession of.

363 *Lord Governor*: Cassio.

364 *censure*: Trial.

PENGUIN SHAKESPEARE

THE WINTER'S TALE
WILLIAM SHAKESPEARE

The jealous King of Sicily becomes convinced that his wife is carrying the child of his best friend. Imprisoned and put on trial, the Queen collapses when the King refuses to accept the divine confirmation of her innocence. The child is abandoned to die on the coast of Bohemia. But when she is found and raised by a shepherd, it seems redemption may be possible.

This book includes a general introduction to Shakespeare's life and the Elizabethan theatre, a separate introduction to *The Winter's Tale*, a chronology of his works, suggestions for further reading, an essay discussing performance options on both stage and screen by Paul Edmondson, and a commentary.

Edited by Ernest Schanzer

With an introduction by Russ McDonald

General Editor: Stanley Wells

Penguin Shakespeare

TIMON OF ATHENS
WILLIAM SHAKESPEARE

After squandering his wealth with prodigal generosity, a rich Athenian gentleman finds himself deep in debt. Unshaken by the prospect of bankruptcy, he is certain that the friends he has helped so often will come to his aid. But when they learn his wealth is gone, he quickly finds that their promises fall away to nothing in this tragic exploration of power, greed, and loyalty betrayed.

This book includes a general introduction to Shakespeare's life and the Elizabethan theatre, a separate introduction to *Timon of Athens*, a chronology of his works, suggestions for further reading, an essay discussing performance options on both stage and screen, and a commentary.

Edited by G. R. Hibbard

With an introduction by Nicholas Walton

General Editor: Stanley Wells

PENGUIN SHAKESPEARE